Is There a Word from the Lord?

Joyce Sibthorpe

New Wine Press

New Wine Press
PO Box 17
Chichester
England PO20 6YB

ISBN: 1-903725-21-6

Typeset by CRB Associates, Reepham, Norfolk.
Printed in England by Clays Ltd, St Ives plc.

Contents

Acknowledgements

Many thanks to all who have helped in the production of this book. To Anne Vyce who typed at breakneck speed to get it on the computer, my husband Charles, who worked with me on the editing and polishing. Alison Kember, Mark Jeffery and Angela Young, all checked and double checked for grammatical errors and made suggestions to help keep the flow.

This book has been written as a response to an instruction given whilst I was in Ghana in October 2002. God told me to have the manuscript finished before Christmas. I have been obedient, but am well aware that in doing so have put pressure on my family and church, especially the Living Waters Church office.

Thank you, you have all been very gracious.

Introduction

Why I have written this book

The Apostle Paul writing in Romans 8:14 states, *'... those who are led by the Spirit of God are sons of God.'* I like to change the word order and say, 'Sons of God are led by the Spirit of God.' But how?

Is it a complicated process for spiritual giants? Can any child of God be 'led'?

How was this demonstrated by Jesus and His disciples? How will it work in our lives today?

Jesus said, *'He who belongs to God hears what God says.'*

Is God still speaking today? Is 'Radio Heaven' still broadcasting? The aim of this book is to answer these questions, to help you to keep tuned to God's wavelength, so that you constantly do what Isaiah 50:4–5 states:

> *'The Master, God, Has given me a well taught tongue, so I know how to encourage tired people. He wakes me up in the morning, wakes me up, opens my ears to listen as one ready to take orders. The Master, God, opened my ears and I didn't go back to sleep, didn't pull the covers back over my head. I followed orders ...'* (*The Message*)

I have drawn from the teaching of the Bible, from my own personal experience and that of others to encourage you to seek God, and to show you how to tune in to God's voice. Your listening ear could be the means of saving life, of enabling you to speak God's word into the lives of others, and to live with a new excitement and purpose that Jesus described as 'abundant life'.

Ten years ago I wrote my first book, *Can You Hear God?*. In it I shared my own adventure in learning how to hear God's voice, how I began, how I practised, how I grew in confidence, and I encouraged you to expect you to hear God, to trust what you heard, and to see God in action.

The book you are now reading unfolds my own learning curve over the next 10 years. It traces failure, as well as success. My great desire is that you will be encouraged and stimulated to get into the action and listen and act at His command.

If you have not read, *Can You Hear God?* I would strongly urge you to get a copy[1] and read it, as I deal with practical issues and teach you different ways of seeking God. It provides foundational teaching that will help you use this book more effectively.

Note

1. For details of how to get a copy of *Can you Hear God?* see page 126.

Chapter 1

God Spoke My Name

It had taken three hours on the train, a couple of bus rides and a half an hour on foot to make the journey, but despite the tiredness she was full of anticipation. Irena (or at least that's what we'll call her) was about to have her first introduction to the Russian underground church at their clandestine gathering deep in the countryside. It was raining, her arms ached with the weight of the small boy she carried, but her heart was beating rapidly with joy and excitement. More than six hundred were gathered in the woods. It was good to worship Jesus out loud; normally they sang 'inside' so as not to risk discovery in the block of flats where they usually met.

The preacher's message had been clear and helpful, and as he gave personal words of encouragement to the people in the crowd, she pushed forward, hoping to be noticed, longing for a word for herself. Irena was a very new believer, and this was the first time she had met with the banned underground church. This was happening at the height of the Cold War, days when fear and suspicion reigned, when believers were imprisoned or sent to far-flung regions of the Soviet Union. All gatherings of Christians were illegal, and those who flouted these laws were in constant danger.

Fellow students, who vouched for her and assured the leadership she was a genuine seeker after God and not a KGB plant, had brought her to the meeting. They had befriended her when she had discovered she was pregnant and cared for her when the father of her child abandoned her.

Her mother had strongly opposed her new found faith and friends with many negative words, but the Spirit of God had drawn her and He had a purpose in her being there in the woods on that particular day. The preacher prophesied for over three hours; suddenly he looked in her direction, his piercing eyes locked with hers and he spoke to her by name.

> 'Little Irena you are so small, smaller than the child you carry in your arms [he was right, she was a baby Christian]. When the great divorce comes you will become as bold as a lion and as strong as an ox.'

She didn't understand. How did he know my name? What did it mean? Why had he spoken to her in that manner? The people around her seemed very excited, but she was confused. Travelling home she discussed the matter with her friends. They explained that the preacher in the woods was a prophet and the words she had heard were a message from God. Questions filled her mind. How did the man know her name? What did the strange words mean? She was not married, so how could she be divorced? His words, however, found a hiding place in her heart and over the next nine years she often recalled them, pondering, trying to make sense of them.

During this time she became a strong Christian believer. There were many difficulties, opposition from her non-Christian mother and poor work situations, but she was sustained by her personal faith and the love of fellow believers. At this time many people were trying to leave the

Soviet block and make their way to the West, travelling via camps in Vienna or Rome, en route to freedom in whatever country would accept them. She had been very surprised, horrified in fact, that some of her close friends, a couple with five children, had written to President Brezhnev and complained they had no religious freedom. They told him they were Pentecostals and they had no liberty to worship as God required. They had asked for permission to leave the country! Their fellow believers were alarmed at what they had done, fearing reprisals, but to everyone's utter amazement the family were granted permission to leave Russia. They were given two provisos; they could take nothing with them and they could never return.

A precedent had been set by 'The Siberian Seven', who after taking refuge in the American Embassy, had been granted permission to leave. It was common knowledge that in these circumstances you had to be ready to go at any moment, often with as little as one day's notice; all part of Soviet harassment. The permits came through, and as anticipated they had only twenty-four hours to say goodbye. The two families had been very close, and now Irena's son would be losing his best friend; the boys were of similar age and had often stayed in each other's homes. The family were leaving everything familiar and there was still the possibility of a last minute change of mind by the authorities. To add to this, not all their relatives were happy with the decision to flee the country.

Irena's flat was full that last night, eight extra people, mother, father, five children and Grandma, who was angry and bitter at losing not only her son, but also her grandchildren. One by one they fell asleep, some in chairs, some on the floor, all exhausted by the emotion of the farewells and the unknown future.

On waking, they discovered that someone was missing. Grandma had dealt treacherously with them and had fled taking her eldest grandson with her. Panic ensued and Irena was dispatched to seek out and find the missing pair, meanwhile the rest of the party, including Irena's son, left for the airport. They had five hours before the flight was due to depart and during that time Irena searched desperately for the missing boy, but to no avail. Exhausted and confused she made her way to the airport, wondering what might happen next. She could never have prepared herself for what she found. The plane had already taken off, the family had gone, and her only son was on the flight. It had been necessary to have five children in order to verify their documentation, and as Irena's son was the same age and a similar size to the missing boy, they smuggled him through as part of the family.

Irena was devastated; the incredible shock overwhelmed her, causing her to become white-haired overnight. Driven by their fanatical desire for freedom they had momentarily cast aside friendship, decency and honesty. They had lied in order to escape, and no one will ever know the agony Irena suffered: not only personal loss and betrayal, but also much mockery from her unbelieving mother as well as endless confrontation and interrogation from the KGB.

Within twenty-four hours she received a phone call from Vienna. She listened as the family asked for forgiveness and explained their actions, then she heard her son's voice, assured him of her love and said she would somehow find a way to come to him. The phone began to crackle as the Soviets sought to jam the line and make communication impossible. Outraged, she found a previously unknown boldness rising up from within her. Irena shouted, 'Get off this line, I will speak to my son, in the Name of Jesus stop this interference.' The line cleared and she continued to reassure the boy of her love for him.

The prophet's word was coming true, 'you will become as bold as a lion.'

But this was only the beginning of the trial she would now endure. It wasn't long before the KGB were questioning her, bullying her, accusing her of killing her own son, even though by now they had substantial evidence of what had really happened.

She immediately applied for permission to leave the country, and in the next ten months embarked upon a remarkable battle with the authorities and the KGB. On one occasion she stood before her accuser and as the Spirit of God came upon her she found herself telling him, 'Today you judge me without mercy and with no justice. You are cruel and ruthless, but one day you will stand before the judge of heaven and earth and He will find you guilty and you will then receive your punishment.' Enraged he commanded her to leave the room, but her words had made their impact.

The conviction of the Holy Spirit came upon him and the next time he examined her, he dismissed his fellow officers and when they were alone he asked her if she remembered her last words to him. She did. He told her that God's judgement had already begun and then he asked her about her faith and she was able to speak freely to him about Jesus and forgiveness.

God moved in many ways on her behalf. She applied for a visa to enter the country of Israel. She hoped eventually to go to Sweden, where she knew her son was now living. The believers made much intercession and eventually permission was granted. A church in Sweden had paid the fare, and now it was her turn to fly towards freedom. While in the transit camp waiting for the 'plane to take her to Israel her papers were checked for a final time and to her amazement she found that, unknown to her, she had already been granted a Swedish visitor's visa, which she had been unable to read. It was within days of running out and just in time she was able to change her flight and go to Sweden, her newly adopted country. There she was reunited with her beloved child.

I met this dear lady twenty years after these events whilst I was in Sweden ministering at a Summer Bible Camp. She translated our English teaching into Russian, so that a group of new believers from Siberia could learn how to hear God.

She told us their remarkable stories, and her own. She now lives in Sweden. She loves to tell how God saw her in the woods, saw the trials she would have to endure and gave her a prophetic word, which at the right time gave her supernatural resources. In fact, her life and hope were sustained by the fact that God had spoken her name and given her an explicit word that carried her through all these adversities.

Important points

- The prophetic word brings strengthening, encouragement and comfort (see 1 Corinthians 14:3).
- God knows you by name.
- When you are weak He has promised you will know His strength.
- Mary treasured the prophetic words given about Jesus and pondered them in her heart. We need to do likewise.
- The prophetic word needs time to reach fulfilment. Keep holding on.

Chapter 2

Tuning in

All believers in Jesus can hear God's voice. Jesus said, *'He who belongs to God hears what God says.'* (John 8:47), and in Amos 4:13, the prophet says, *'He who forms the mountains, creates the wind, and reveals his thoughts to man.'*

Voices are very distinctive; you can instantly recognise someone you have not heard for many years, even over the telephone. There is also something about the tone of a voice that enables you to detect sadness, joy and pain and other emotions, as well as enthusiasm or authority. A person you know well can be speaking in different roles and the tone of voice will enable you to distinguish which one. It was reported that Princess Anne, when questioned about her relationship with the Queen, replied, 'She is my mother, but she is always the Queen.'

God is always God, but He can speak to us intimately as our Father, tenderly as the Comforter and strongly as the one who disciplines and corrects. At times there is an urgent note in His voice, or He may make us laugh as He talks with us as a friend. If your relationship with God has been formal, you may need to learn about intimacy; if you have known God as a loving Father, but not as the Most High God, you may need to acknowledge that He is awesome and bow in reverence before such a God, There are times when God is speaking, as

Almighty God and I need to physically stand before Him, at other times I am happy to relax and sit at His feet.

The written words of the Bible

The Bible is the Word of God. 2 Timothy 3:16 states that it is given for teaching, rebuking, correcting, training in righteousness and equipping us for every good work. The Word of God is a living book and speaks today as it has throughout history with clarity and authority. I read the whole Bible through each year using a Bible Reading Plan.[1] I like to read it in many translations, not wanting to become too familiar with one version and thus lose the impact of its message. As I read well-known passages in a fresh text I am provoked and stimulated. I want the Holy Spirit to catch my attention, so that I see things I haven't seen before.

The Holy Spirit is always the one who brings understanding and revelation. I often find that a certain verse or phrase seems to jump out from the page and hit me straight between the eyes. This is when God takes part of His written Word and makes it alive for me at that moment. It may bring new direction, or give me peace in a time of crisis. It may have been written two thousand years ago, but in that instant it is a new, living and prophetic word for me at a time of particular need.

Open my eyes

I pray Ephesians 1:18 every time I read the Word of God because I want the eyes of my understanding to be enlightened, and Psalm 119:18, which says, *'Open my eyes that I may see wonderful things in your law.'* Recently I was reading a passage containing the words *'The Most High God'*. Yes, I know God is my Father, but do I know Him as 'The Most High God'? I began to explore this further. I have a Bible with cross-references and after having marked this phrase, I looked at the other places in Scripture where God is described as 'The Most High God', and through this I learned new things, which challenged me. I also keep a journal of what I am learning and review this regularly.

Knowing the real thing

One question that I am often asked is, 'How can I know that what I am hearing is really the voice of God?'

In order to detect forged bank notes you concentrate on the real thing; the more familiar you become with the original the more clearly you detect the counterfeit. In a similar way the more you know the Word of God, the more easily you detect anything bogus. A word of caution: never let the prophetic voice of the Spirit become a substitute for regular and consistent reading of the Word of God. We need both. If you are not familiar with the written Word you could be in danger of being deceived. Consistent reading of the original will guard you from the counterfeit.

My husband knows me very well; if someone told him that I had said 'such and such' he would immediately know whether I had or not. He knows me, he knows how I think, how I speak. Such knowledge would soon uncover anything false, and he would confidently say, 'Joyce would never say anything like that.' Our plumb-line is the canon of Scripture. It is our safeguard. God will not speak by His Spirit things that are contrary to His Word. 2 Timothy 2:15 urges:

> *'Study to show yourself approved unto God, a workman who has no need to be ashamed, rightly handling the word of truth.'*

The inner voice of the Holy Spirit

Tune in to the Holy Spirit speaking from the place where your conscience speaks.

Ask yourself how you hear that inner voice of conscience that challenges you about right and wrong. Where do you hear it? What does it sound like? How do you know? This knowing place is important. God's Spirit speaks in a similar way to conscience. You will know that deep inner conviction that there is something wrong and that you are disturbed or have that inner settled assurance that you have peace. Hearing from God is the development of this inner voice of conscience. Take time to listen carefully and you will not only have a sense of disquiet or peace, but you will hear in greater detail what God is saying.

Outside voices that can capture your attention

If you are alert you can become sensitive to any number of ways God may use to speak to you. It could be a preacher, a friend or a book. Their words may disturb you and cause you to ask questions. When this happens, go back to God and ask if He is trying to speak to you. It may be things that you see in normal everyday life. You may have walked past a certain gateway a thousand times, but this time you notice it, it is imprinted on your mind. God may well be asking you, what do you see? God asked many of the prophets this question. Jeremiah saw an almond branch as God spoke to him (Jeremiah 1:11). Amos saw a basket of ripe fruit (Amos 8:1), Moses a burning bush (Exodus 3:1–3). You may see visions and pictures or dreams. You may have deep impressions in your spirit that will not go away, or be aware of feeling heightened emotions such as grief or pain as you look into someone's face. Is God trying to get your attention? Does He want to speak to you about this situation? The advice Samuel, the trainee prophet, was given by Eli, the Old Testament priest of Israel, still holds good,

> *'Speak, Lord, for your servant is listening.'* (1 Samuel 3:9)

Ask questions as you listen

King David asked many times: shall I do this or that?

> *'... he inquired of the LORD, saying, "Shall I go and attack these Philistines?" The LORD answered him, "Go, attack the Philistines and save Keilah."'* (1 Samuel 23:2)

Some of you will hear God's direction as you bring a set of circumstances before Him in prayer. You may ask the question, 'If I do this, will You be pleased?' You may re-run the scenario and feel a greater peace having approached these things differently. Colossian 3:15 says:

> *'Let the peace of Christ rule in your hearts.'*

The greek word rendered here 'rule', is commonly used in reference to the Olympic and other games, it means 'to preside or sit as umpire'. Peace will be the umpire in your life; listen for its presence or absence.

What if I have ignored His voice in the past?

You may be aware that God has spoken to you in the past and you have ignored what He has said or deliberately disobeyed Him. You need to ask His forgiveness for this. Jonah, the Old Testament prophet, did just this and when he had repented, the Word of the Lord came to him a second time. (See Jonah 3:1.)

An audible voice

God does speak in an external audible voice. Saul heard it on the Damascus road (Acts 9:4). Jesus heard it at His baptism (Luke 2:22), at His transfiguration (Matthew 17:5), and just before the crucifixion (John 12:28). Others have heard God speak in this way, when He has given them life-changing commissions with far reaching results. However, most of the time God speaks to us it will be through *'the still small voice'* of His Holy Spirit and it is this voice we will be exploring. 'Radio heaven' is always broadcasting; we need to switch on our receivers and tune in to the signal.

Hearing God without really knowing it!

Henry Sibthorpe, my late father-in-law, would not have been familiar with hearing God in the ways I am describing. He was a man of God, who knew and loved God's written Word, the Bible. He did however hear God's voice many times and in different ways without knowing it. Here is one example. Henry was amazingly good at calligraphy; he had perfected this art form and produced many fine examples. He had inscribed the place settings at his grand-daughter's wedding. They looked beautiful and many guests commented on them. Once they had discovered the 80-year-old calligrapher, they wanted to see him demonstrate his craft. So he simply took the name place card, looked at the person who was giving it to him and wrote a Bible verse on the back. He was in fact giving each one a living word from God. As these guests read their Bible verse they were astounded at the appropriateness of each text. Henry thought he was demonstrating his calligraphy, but he was giving words from heaven. Recently I was at a family gathering in Germany; many people asked after Henry and reminded me of this occasion. Some of these people are not yet Christians. One person told me: I still have the place setting your father-in-law inscribed for me, and it has brought such hope to me.

As you read this book, my desire is that you will grow in confidence and know that you are hearing God's voice and the boldness to speak His word to others. Please read all the passages I quote from Scripture. Jesus knew His Scriptures very well, He quite often argued from them, relied on their promises, and repeated the miracles. We need to do the same.

Psalm 81 talks about God's longing for His people to listen to Him, and it gives promises for those who do. Read it and find out what you will gain by listening.

Important points

- If you belong to God you can hear what He says. Don't speak any words that contradict this truth.
- Develop consistent daily reading of the Bible.
- Identify your way of hearing.
- Have the confidence to write down and speak out what you hear.
- Slow down, look, listen. God is always speaking. Don't miss it.

Note

1. For details of how to get a copy of *The Workman's Bible Reading Plan* see page 126.

Chapter 3

Are You Using *All* Your Senses?

You can 'listen' with your other senses as well as your spiritual ears. God can use every sense and physical faculty to speak to you and get your attention. Never limit God. He's full of surprises and is always creative in His actions. We're the boring ones who will try to reduce everything to a formula.

Symptoms, but not yours

Charles will often identify people's healing needs by feeling physical discomfort in his own body. The first time this happened he was ministering in Sweden. He told the people present, 'God is going to heal tonight and He will show me where He is going to begin.' Immediately he felt a stiffness and pain in two fingers on his right hand, the ring and the little finger. He spoke this out very specifically. He didn't just say, 'There's somebody here with a hand injury.' No, he drew attention to the exact place where he was experiencing the pain. A man responded and told how he'd been involved in an agricultural accident and had severed the tendons in those specific fingers. Doctors had told him that there was nothing that could be done and he would have to live with the disability for the rest of his life. As his symptoms were described, faith was quickened in his heart and he received healing. At the end of the meeting, he came to the front, sat at the piano and began to worship God. His great delight had been to play the piano, which he had been unable to do for the previous two years because of this injury.

That night another lady was healed as Charles described symptoms of severe pain in his neck. She'd had a whiplash injury, which had been prayed for many times, but with no tangible result. She was sceptical, thought this was possibly a word to encourage her faith, but wasn't sure. When some weeks later she was free of all pain and discomfort she traced the healing back to that night.

Charles will usually give such words when ministering at the end of a meeting. When it seems that he has finished, he will check his body again, and if he still has, say, toothache, he will give the word of knowledge again. There may be someone who is having great difficulty in believing the word and when the location of the pain is very specific this helps to release faith in God's healing power.

When all painful symptoms have gone, it is usually an indication that each has been received by faith, and that God's healing power is in action, even though all healings may not be instantaneous.

Drive quickly, the pain is severe

Julian Perkins, a friend and an elder at Living Waters Church, had for many years suffered bouts of sciatica which were excruciatingly painful and debilitating. He once was unable to work for six weeks. Much prayer had been made, pleading with God to heal this back. Medical examination and treatment had failed to bring relief. After an attack and enforced bed rest he would recover enough to work, but pain was never far away and he experienced numbness in his leg as a result of this trapped sciatic nerve.

It's hard to sustain faith for healing when you have a long-term condition. You want to believe, and mentally you do, but continued disappointment undermines your faith. It is into this kind of situation that God gives words of knowledge to encourage faith.

Ian Andrews, a minister with a profoundly powerful healing anointing, was staying in our home at a time when Julian was flat on his back and couldn't move. We knew he was very upset that he would have to miss the ministry training session that Ian was to lead that night. We phoned Julian and asked whether he would like Ian to pray with him before the evening meeting. He agreed, but with little enthusiasm, because of past disappointments.

As they were on the way to Julian's home, Ian began to experience intense pain, sweating with the agony of it all. He said to Charles, 'Drive quickly. If Julian is in as much pain as I am, we can't get there soon enough.' On arrival at the house Ian told Julian exactly where the pain was, put his hand on the specific place and using the name of Jesus released him from all pain.

Julian sat up, pain free. Hallelujah! His leg was still numb, but after more prayer that was also healed. Ian and Charles were ready to leave for the evening meeting, when Julian said, 'Hang on, wait for me.' He got dressed, came to the meeting, testified to his healing, and has been well, and pain free with no further occurrence for over two years.

Feeling emotional pain

Another lady, who is a member of Living Waters Church, feels emotions. She will be sitting in a room and start feeling intense fear, bordering on panic. Not being a fearful person herself, she will look round to see if she can spot someone who might be experiencing this trauma. Sometimes she knows who it is, other times she will speak out what she is feeling and ask, 'Is there anyone here who is feeling like this?' She will then pray and release God's healing and peace into their situation.

Very recently she was sitting beside someone in a prayer meeting and experienced such emotional pain, she felt as if she was raw inside. This was not physical pain, rather a wound of the heart. She turned to the person and said, 'This pain is awful, let me pray for you.' The person concerned was not at all willing to receive prayer, and said so. She didn't want a fuss; she didn't want to draw attention to herself, so she said, 'You can pray for me, but not now.'

My friend simply said, 'God didn't cause this wound.' That word was received and later, as this lady was going to bed she simply said, 'I know it wasn't you, God, who did it.' She fell asleep and woke free from pain, free from disappointment, free to move on, free to let go of all that had wounded her.

Discerning motivating forces

Another friend senses the motivating emotion behind a person's actions or words. Sometimes it speaks so loudly – of hate, say – that she can't hear anything of what they are saying.

Seeing more than meets the eyes

Another time Charles was ministering in Burundi to a sea of black faces. Suddenly he saw the features of a familiar white English face superimposed on the black face in front of him. The face he was looking at was of a young man who had been severely addicted to cocaine and, sadly, had died as a result of drug abuse. This vision shocked Charles and he spoke out a warning to this man, and prayed for him to be released from addiction.

Bloodhound instincts

There are times, while ministering, when I detect significant smells and believe that God is speaking to me through my sense of smell.

Sometimes I will smell alcohol or tobacco as I pray for someone. That person may not be currently drinking or smoking; they may even have been eating mints. This happened one time when I was praying for a man with a cough who had also lost his voice. I was almost overwhelmed by the smell of tobacco, but he had not smoked for more than six months. He was wearing clean clothes, so the smell was not hanging around him that way. The Holy Spirit revealed the source of his condition was connected with his past smoking habit, and again he was set free and healed.

God uses this ability to smell to prevent me praying for an obvious symptom, when God wants to heal something much deeper and more important.

There is a smell associated with demons, and evil and unclean spirits. In fact there is a man in our church who has lost his natural sense of smell but can still smell the demonic. There is also a sweet fragrance, which comes from the Holy Spirit. I have been in gatherings when God's presence has been very real, and I have been aware of a floral smell so sweet and powerful when there have been no flowers in the building, and the aroma was unlike any manufactured perfume. Jesus is described as the 'Lily of the Valley' and the 'Rose of Sharon' and when He is in a place it is possible to know it because of the sweetness of His fragrance.

Seeing or hearing

It is most likely that we develop our sensitivity in perhaps only one or two of these areas. We all have natural preferences and will be more comfortable using one of our senses than another. I personally enjoy listening more than looking, so I will listen to audiotapes in preference to watching videos. If I have a video on the VCR, I will often do something else at the same time, like knitting or ironing. My concentration is on the audio, not the visual, and this preference is reflected in the fact that I hear more from the Holy Spirit than I see.

For others it is different. Their 'eye gate' is more sensitive than their 'ear gate', so they will see visions and dream dreams. God's communication skills are infinite and inventive. Be alert.

However, there have been times when God has spoken to me in visions. Recently I was in Ghana and whilst in prayer I saw a flash picture in my mind of a young African girl. In the snapshot, she had her back to me, and was bending down, stirring a pot, wearing a yellow skirt and top. The skirt was Western style, straight with a split to the knees at the back, and I could see her brown legs, but not her face. To be honest, as I saw this, I didn't even pray about it; it was just fixed in my mind for a few seconds.

Three days later I was some miles away in the garden of a house in Kumasi. I was sitting under a tree, talking to a pastor's wife and as I looked up towards her house there was exactly the same picture that I had seen three days earlier, but this time in reality.

I asked about the girl, called her to me, and told her that Jesus had shown her to me in a vision about three days before, wearing exactly the clothes she now had on. I said, 'He must be searching for you. You must be one of His lost sheep.' She was, and that day she was found.

That was the first time I had seen with such clarity in quite this way; it was so specific, and led to that girl meeting Jesus. I am expecting God to show me more of those that He is looking for.

Cartoons

God speaks to some people in cartoons. I recently met a lady whose journal was full of such drawings. They had been given as she asked questions and sought God for wisdom. As she listens, clear images appear in her mind which she then draws 'cartoon style' in her notebook. They always contain helpful and creative insights.

A lady in our church is training to navigate ocean-going yachts and was finding the trigonometry very taxing. At the point of giving up she asked God to speak, He gave her one word in the form of a cartoon. She saw this in her mind in bright yellow letters. It made her laugh and gain perspective, and as she obeyed the word she found the task much easier. The word was 'enjoy', but it was given in this form.

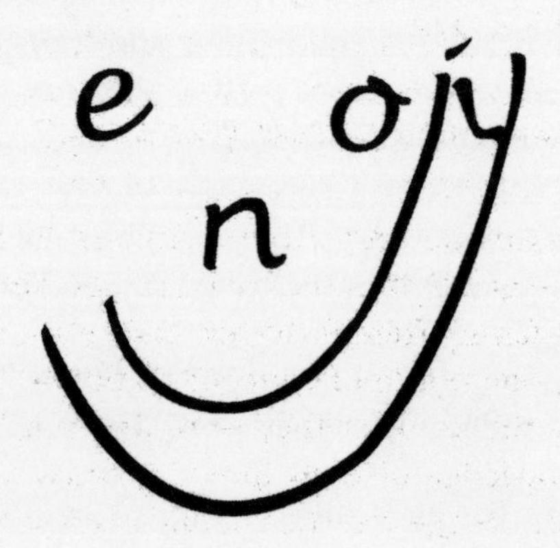

Dreams

God speaks clearly through dreams. So often we dismiss them as too much cheese or pizza the night before. I used to think like this until about six years ago I met friends in Galway to whom God spoke clearly and directively though their dreams. I asked them to pray for me. I don't want to lie unproductively asleep for six hours if God can speak while I am horizontal.

Since then I have recorded significant dreams and asked God for interpretations and He has spoken many times through my dreams. In Numbers 12:6–8 God says:

> *'When a prophet of the* LORD *is among you,*
> *I reveal myself to him in visions,*
> *I speak to him in dreams.*
> *But this is not true of my servant Moses;*
> *he is faithful in all my house.*
> *With him I speak face to face.'*

I keep a pad beside my bed and write down significant dreams; I then pray and ask the Holy Spirit if he is speaking to me. Daniel 7:2 says:

> *'He wrote down the substance of his dream.'*

My daughter Coralie rang from Germany to tell me of a dream that had greatly troubled her. She described the details that involved family friends. In her dream these two people kept opening one bottle of wine after another, and she felt concerned by the amount they were drinking. She had no first-hand knowledge of their lifestyle, and asked me what she should do. I suggested she should to pray, ask God why she had been given this dream, and enquire whether there was any action she ought to take. She prayed, and decided she needed to communicate with them. The dream was recounted without comment, and they received it as a warning, without feeling judged or criticised, as there was something pure and simple about it. It had sounded a necessary caution, had come from a pure source at the right moment and was a word in season.

Important points

- Stir up the gifts where you have some experience. Use what you've got.
- Learn from more experienced people. Ask, 'How do you hear?' 'How does that work?' 'What do you mean by that?' Those are the sorts of questions that I learned to ask.
- Trust the Holy Spirit; don't be afraid to experiment.
- When God activates a new sense for you – press in and expect more.

Chapter 4

Alone with God

In order to achieve intimacy in a relationship, many things are required. You need time alone, undisturbed by interruptions, a quiet place, a safe place, somewhere where you can relax and share your heart and be open and transparent, where your raw emotions can spill out without being judged.

In a similar way we need to find that safe place in God. It may start as a safe and quiet physical place, but it ultimately must become an internal place where you meet Jesus, the Lover of your soul.

Jesus knew how to spend time with God

Jesus knew how to go to the quiet place and meet with His Father. He discovered it as a child and it was to become an essential part of His communication with His Father. As a boy of twelve, He had stayed behind in Jerusalem after His family had set off for home. He wanted to be in His Father's house where *'everyone who heard him was amazed at his understanding and his answers.'* This was a twelve-year-old, but He had already forged His relationship with His Heavenly Father. When Mary and Joseph eventually found Him, the surprised response they received was, *'Didn't you know I had to be in My Father's house?'*

Jesus had been conceived and brought to birth by the Holy Spirit, who was already teaching Him, but He had to grow in wisdom, stature and favour with God and man; He had to learn obedience and how to find God in the common, mundane things of life. When He began to teach publicly, at the age of thirty, the crowd was amazed at His teaching; He spoke with authority, the authority of someone who knows His God. They were greatly puzzled as to where He had received this teaching.

John 3:31–32 says:

> *'The One who comes from above is head and shoulders over other messengers from God. The earthborn is earthbound and speaks earth language; the heavenborn is in a league of his own. He sets out the evidence of what he saw and heard in heaven.'* (*The Message*)

Think about the many times when Jesus withdrew from the crowds to a quiet place to pray. Sometimes He needed to spend nights in prayer; His place was mountains, away from it all, they became some of His favourite retreats, as did the olive grove near Bethany.

You need to find where you can be alone with God. Do you have such a place?

A lonely schoolgirl learns intimacy

After I was saved at the age of eleven, circumstances dictated that I spent a great deal of time on my own. In term time I was at boarding school, but in the school holidays, as my mother had a full-time job, I spent many days on my own. To start off with I didn't appreciate the loneliness. I moaned and groaned to God that life was so unfair. Why didn't I have a normal, family life like others? It was then that I learned to know God. I had time to read and time to pour out my heart to God. I learned to identify very much with David, the psalmist, who was not afraid to admit despair, cry it all out to God, get peace, and then rejoice and declare again that God is good.

As I look back to that very difficult time, I see that it was then that I forged a real relationship with God and came to know Him, to desire Him and walk with Him and He placed me on the pathway that I still walk today. To develop this intimacy with God is my abiding passion, and I am always wanting to learn more about seeking Him and drawing closer.

Learn from others

Over the years I have had the privilege of meeting hundreds of God's servants. I can always recognise those who know their God, many of them better than I, and have constantly sought to learn from them. In the early days of our marriage we had a large house and we were able to offer hospitality to many people. It became a pattern of life to host visiting speakers who were teaching at events in West Cornwall. I was so hungry to know more of God, and especially to find people who were following the Holy Spirit and who had greater experience of spiritual gifts. Each time a new person came I would immediately distinguish between those who knew God and those who only knew about Him. The former radiated a sweetness, a depth, something that spoke of a man or woman who had an intimate walk with God.

I remember one man, a student at a Bible College, who was ill during the time he stayed with us. Even taking a cup of tea into his room was a privilege because Jesus was there; he had a lifestyle of prayer and fasting; he had a secret place. I almost felt as if I was intruding, and I have never forgotten the effect of seeing this.

Arthur Wallis, a pioneer in the move of the Holy Spirit, stayed with us for a week and it was like having Jesus in the house. We laughed together, it was such fun. Arthur was so patient with us, and as we would talk together after a meeting, and bombard him with questions, he explaining carefully what we needed to understand. He was so very honest as we barged into areas where angels feared to tread.

I questioned him about his ministry. 'Was he an evangelist, a teacher?' 'No, a prophet.' 'A what?' In 1969 there weren't many of them. 'And how do you become a prophet? Who told you that you were a prophet?' Never-ending, innocent questions from me. Endless, patient answers from Arthur; words of wisdom and impartation that are remembered even thirty years later. He had been taught by God and was imparting to us. Arthur was always up hours before us, wonderfully human, but at all times in touch with his Heavenly Father.

Denis Clark, another man of God, who had formerly worked with Youth for Christ in South Africa but had come to England to carry responsibility for European Youth for Christ, was a man with a huge heart, big family and 'say it as it is' mouth. Again, he was so much fun to be with, the source of much practical wisdom. An intercessor who co-founded Intercessors for Britain, he was equally at home demonstrating a miracle cleaning product. Late one night I remember him getting sticky finger marks off the wall of our stairs, chanting the product's logo, 'One wipe with Swipe takes the rubbing out of scrubbing'. We bought his products; we also took much practical child-rearing advice from him. Every month he sent out a newsletter and we couldn't wait to hear what Denis had written. It was always fresh bread, straight from heaven. These were giants who knew their God and they did exploits; they pioneered the move of God we now freely live in; they knew how to be alone and receive from God, and we knew they had something worth listening to.

I want to be a person who is taught by God, who will have the same influence on people I meet, and I want this for you. Get alone with your Heavenly Father and He will teach you and lead you into all truth. John 15:15 says:

> *'I no longer call you servants, because a servant does not know his master's business. Instead, I have called you friends, for everything that I learned from my Father I have made known to you.'*

John 16:12–16 says:

> *'I have much more to say to you, more than you can now bear. But when he, the Spirit of truth, comes, he will guide you into all truth. He will not speak on his own; he will speak only what he hears, and he will tell you what is yet to come. He will bring glory to me by taking from what is mine and making it known to you. All that belongs to the Father is mine. That is why I said the Spirit will take from what is mine and make it known to you.'*

Those in prison

You may find that you are in prison because of breaking the law and you are restricted in your freedom. You may have an enforced time of aloneness, but you can meet with God right where you are. I know at least three men who have met with God in the way I have described, whilst in prison. They are men whom I respect, forgiven men. They have taken the punishment they deserved, but God had to get them still long enough to talk to them, to meet with them and to change them. They had met with God in one of the hardest places. He will come wherever He is invited and He isn't ashamed of a prison cell. It could turn into your Bible College, it could be the best time of your life.

The seasons of life

Life moves in seasons; when my own children were small I found it almost impossible to get alone with God. The desire was there but the reality very different. At that time Denis Clark, who I mentioned earlier, came to stay with us. He had five children so he understood the scenario. I was very tired and he just said to me, 'Joyce, are you having time alone with God?' I wasn't, and I justified myself, gave him excuses, and told him why I couldn't. Then he turned to my husband and he said, 'Charles, you've got to enable her to have time on her own with God.'

We sat down, we evaluated how this could happen and we agreed that we would get up, Charles would do the children's breakfast, and I would go to the furthest part of the house so that I couldn't hear the noise they were making, where I would seek to have at least a short time with God.

It wasn't easy. It was a decision of the will, it had to be planned, and I had to choose to do it. I could often hear the chaos going on downstairs and I would think, 'Oh, I can't stay here I'll go and sort it out.' But God would say to me, 'No, you let them sort it out. You stay here with Me.'

We have to be practical. And it may be that you are at that stage of life where the pressure of children, family, business, work are all demanding of you, but you need to carve out time with your Heavenly Father because it's in His presence that we find rest, that we find refreshment.

Where do you go?

So, where do you go to be alone with God? Where do you feel the most relaxed and safe? Go there. Have you been there recently? May be that's why you feel so weary.

> *'But those who wait on the* L*ORD*

Shall renew their strength;
They shall mount up with wings like eagles,
They shall run and not be weary,
They shall walk and not faint.' (Isaiah 40:31 NKJV)

Ask God to let you meet with Him like this. It might be 'walking the dog' time alone with God. It might be 'cutting the grass' time alone with God. It might be in the car without a radio, tape or CD. God knows the pace of life we all live and He knows about time pressure, but if you want to know your God, you will have to find a place where you can be alone with Him.

God spoke out His longing for intimacy with His people in Hosea 2:14:

'Therefore I am now going to allure her;
I will lead her into the desert
and speak tenderly to her.'

Important points

- You need to have a daily appointment with God in your secret place.
- Choose to withdraw from the noise and the crowd so that you can get to know Him better.
- Talk to those who have greater experience than you and learn their secrets.
- Remember that God always wants to meet with you in the quiet place. Don't keep Him waiting or fail to keep the appointment.

Chapter 5

Making Mistakes

I was staying with my daughter and family in Germany, when I awoke with a start from a deep sleep. I had been disturbed by a very clear but puzzling dream. Now I lay in bed recalling the details.

In the dream I was wearing my normal walking shoes; familiar, good, sturdy lace-up shoes. I had one shoe on correctly and the other only half on with the back crushed down. An authoritative voice had woken me with the command, 'Put these shoes on properly!' I was ready with my answer, 'I always put them on properly, I don't wear them like that.' I then heard the voice again, 'You didn't tonight.' Now I was really awake, 'Please, will You speak to me, will You correct me, Father?' I recognised the voice of my Father God and I was alert and ready for His correction. I know God disciplines those He loves, just as a good, earthly father will correct and teach his child.

This time God had chosen to use a dream. I saw and was offended by the way these shoes had been worn with the back being broken down, and put on so sloppily. In just the same way, God was offended by my carelessness and needed to correct me.

During the previous evening, I had been asked to visit a couple who had been married for a few years, but as yet were childless. They wanted to receive prayer and hear from heaven. What did God want to say to them about their situation? Did He want them to have children? They were in the region of 40 years of age. Would they be more available and useful to God without a natural family? These were some of the questions they were asking and wanted me to help them to hear what God might be saying.

Earlier in the day I had been talking to my daughter and her husband about several couples in their church that were having difficulty in conceiving and others who had miscarried. We also discussed the decrease in fertility amongst young married couples in Germany today and talked about curses and blessings.

This whole topic of conversation was fresh in my mind, but the Bible clearly says, *'Lean not on your own understanding'* (Proverbs 3:5) and that, sadly, is what I did.

Exodus 23:25 declares:

> *'Worship the LORD your God, and his blessing will be on your food and water. I will take away sickness from among you, and none will miscarry or be barren in your land. I will give you a full lifespan.'*

Part of the covenant blessing in the Old Testament was fruitfulness, and so I went to visit and pray, quite sure that they were experiencing some sort of limiting curse. I listened to them, and we prayed. I broke any curses off them, any national curses, prayed for blessing, and prayed that the womb would open.

I thought I had done quite a good job, until 3am, when God spoke to me and told me that I had my shoes on in a sloppy manner. The Lord continued to speak to me in detail. Did He direct me to pray in the way I did, or had I used experience and human wisdom? Did I love the couple that I was ministering to enough to listen and be honest? Did I have something to prove? Did I need to have all the answers? Inadvertently I had done all of those things – I had not been alert, not ready for walking, not ready for action. Oh dear, did I repent? You bet I did! And quickly, and not quietly!

Experience is not without its value. I have known many situations where curses have caused barrenness, where wombs have been opened as curses have been broken. Galatians chapter 3 teaches us that Jesus took every curse, as he became a curse for us on the cross, so that every curse can be broken and you and I can go free. I have ministered these scriptures and I have seen God release and heal people, as curses have been exchanged for blessing. However, I assumed I knew what was needed, I trusted in experience, barged in without waiting for God's analysis of the situation, and He was not pleased with me. I repented and asked Him what I should do now.

I had left the couple in peace, and had prayed for God's blessing and best purpose for them. I was quite prepared to lose face and repent publicly, but God was gracious to me. I had taken my rebuke, hopefully learned my lesson, and because God's heart is always towards all His children, He didn't want my inadequacy to rob them of their peace. I heard no further instructions from God, so was happy to let the matter rest.

They are, in the natural, childless, but in God they are a Mother and Father in Israel, greatly used by God in His plans and purposes, able to do many things because they are free of the restrictions of family life; happy, fulfilled and I believe they have God's best for them.

Learning lessons

I learned that a curse could easily come on me. You see, I had trusted the arm of the flesh and not the voice of the Spirit. Listen to the words from Jeremiah chapter 17:

'"Cursed is the one who trusts in man,
who depends on flesh for his strength
and whose heart turns away from the LORD.
He will be like a bush in the wastelands;
and he will not see prosperity when it comes.
He will dwell in the parched places of the desert,
in the salt land where no one lives.
But blessed is the man who trusts in the LORD,
whose confidence is in Him.
He will be like a tree planted by the water,
that sends out its roots by the stream.
It does not fear when heat comes;
its leaves are always green.
It has no worries in a year of drought
and never fails to bear fruit."

The heart is deceitful above all things
and beyond cure.
Who can understand it?

"I, the LORD, search the heart
and examine the mind,
to reward a man according to his conduct,
according to what his deeds deserve."'

(Jeremiah 17:5–10)

And as I hear that I am rebuked. Again and again God has needed to ask me whether I am walking by the Spirit or trusting the arm of the flesh? If we are still sense-ruled instead of Spirit-ruled, we will over-ride what God says with the voice of experience, or the voice of past success. If I am not listening to the voice of the Spirit, then I must be listening to the voice of the flesh.

I repented very quickly and thanked God for His rebuke, because I know that I am His child and that He cares for me and rebukes me, because He wants me to learn. The inventor Edison was under great pressure over his repeated failures to invent the electric light bulb. As he was questioned about each failure, he replied every time, 'That's not a failure, that's an education.'

I determined, with God's help, never to act so foolishly again. I want to be quick to listen and slow to speak. Proverbs 15:5 says:

> *'... whoever heeds correction shows prudence.'*

Proverbs 15:32 says:

> *'He who ignores discipline despises himself,*
> *but whoever heeds correction gains understanding.'*

1 Samuel 15:22–26 speaks about 'heeding correction' and the key verse is *'to obey is better than sacrifice and to heed better than the fat of rams.'* Listen to the definition of 'heed':

- To heed is to pay careful attention, to have careful observation, to regard intently, to take careful notice of, to give full attention to, to be watchful or mindful.

And 'heedless' is 'paying no attention, careless and regardless'.

God wants us to be those who will 'heed'. So ask God to bring to remembrance situations where you've acted out of experience and with human wisdom. Repent and ask God for the grace to 'heed' the voice of His Spirit. When we hear the voice from heaven and obey those instructions we will see gates of brass open.

Naturally we do not like admitting we get things wrong. Our human reaction is to blame others or justify our actions. God seems to need to correct me so many times, but He continues to do so because He wants me to change, He is committed to help me rely totally on Him and not on my own wisdom or experience.

Important points

- Do not prejudge any situation.
- Always ask God to speak to you as you listen to others.
- The obvious can often mask the real issue.
- Admitting you can be wrong is a strength, not a weakness.

Chapter 6

A Word from Heaven

The God who speaks

God is a speaking God – He desires intimacy with His children and when we draw near to Him He promises that He will draw near to us. In James 4:8 it says:

> *'Draw near to God and He will draw near to you.'* (NKJV)

As we come to Him He wants to share His heart, His feelings, His emotions, His thoughts, His directions, and His insights. He wants intimacy. Jeremiah 23:22 says,

> *'But if they had stood in my counsel,*
> *they would have proclaimed my words to my people*
> *and would have turned them from their evil ways*
> *and from their evil deeds.'*

Jeremiah 32:33 says:

> *'They turned their backs to me and not their faces; though I taught them again and again, they would not listen . . . '*

One clear, directive word from God can change a person's life. That's why the Bible says in Proverbs 3:5:

> *'... and lean not on your own understanding;*
> *in all your ways acknowledge him,*
> *and he will make your paths straight.'*

On one occasion Jesus was discussing with His disciples who the people thought He was; He then turned to Peter and asked, *'Who do you say I am?'* Peter answered, *'You are the Christ, the Son of the living God.'* This declaration didn't come out of his mind, but rather from a deeper place, right from his insides, a gut reaction. I think it probably took him by surprise. Jesus' comment was *'for this was not revealed to you by man, but by my Father in heaven.'* Peter hadn't thought it out; he just seemed to blurt it out. This is an example of what is called 'revelation knowledge'. The Bible says that the gates of hell will not be able to stand against it; it is a word from heaven.

It's all gone wrong

My husband Charles had a similar experience. The words just popped out of his mouth, and he was so surprised at their simplicity and profoundness that he immediately grabbed a pen and paper and recorded them before they were forgotten.

This is how it happened. We had been helping a lady over a period of time who had been bound by fears and wounds, and who God had wonderfully released and healed. But one morning as she arrived at our house she was looking very sad and downhearted. 'It's all gone wrong, it doesn't work, I've lost my freedom, and I'm in a mess again.'

Charles was under pressure, as he was just about to leave the house for another appointment and there was scarcely any time for talking and questioning. Suddenly words rose from deep within him and he said,

> 'If you want to be free, you can be free. And if you're not free, it's because of one of these four things. It's Unforgiveness, Disobedience, Unconfessed Sin or Believing the Lies of the enemy. If there is someone you haven't forgiven, forgive. If there is something you haven't obeyed, obey. If you know of sin you haven't confessed, confess it now. Or, if you're believing the enemy's lies, start believing what God says in His word. Your problem will be in one of these areas. These are your keys to freedom – use them.'

We soon discovered she had been offended, had failed to forgive and as a result had lost her joy and sense of God's presence. The enemy made sure she felt a failure, and then followed feelings of rejection, and the spiral of negative emotions had quickly deepened. When she heard Charles' words she quickly forgave. From that moment onwards, we only had to say to her 'Check your keys,' and she would be able to identify the devil's strategy quickly and apply the antidote.

Learning to listen before speaking

Some years ago, I was part of a team running a summer family camp, called 'Eagle Camp'. About 1,000 people would gather for a week of teaching, fellowship and fun in the presence of the Lord. On the last night there was always celebration and great rejoicing over the good things that God had done. We would clear away the chairs and the people would dance as the worship band led rapturous praises to God. We were inside a large marquee, in open countryside in summer, so there was plenty of dust and pollen in the atmosphere.

On one such night, I was at the front when a very anxious lady summoned me, 'You must come now, there's a young boy who's having an asthma attack. He can't breathe and we can't help him. Come, come quickly.'

I made my way back through the throng and soon saw a small group surrounding the boy, praying earnestly. He was in a very bad state, grasping for breath, his chest heaving and his heart pounding. I could feel this as I placed my hand on him.

'I' went straight into action. Note the 'I', and 'I' started to pray in tongues and say 'In the Name of Jesus.' Almost immediately, and certainly before I could get out the words 'be healed', I heard the Holy Spirit say, 'Stop, listen to Me.'

At that moment I felt God break in and give me clear instructions and simple steps to follow. 'Ask this boy if he speaks in tongues.'

'Oh God,' I protested inside, 'is that relevant right now? He can't breathe, let alone speak in tongues.'

'Ask him if he can speak in tongues.'

Again, the Holy Spirit prompted me, so I asked the question.

He indicated 'No.' At this stage he couldn't speak. He was using all his strength trying to breathe.

I then asked him 'Do you know Jesus? Is He living in you?'

'Yes, yes,' came the nod of his head.

He was beseeching me to do something quickly. I could see him thinking 'Stop asking stupid questions.'

Then the directive came from heaven, 'Tell him this – you are going to lay your hands on him, he is going to be filled with the Holy Spirit and immediately he will open his mouth and speak in a heavenly language. This language will release praise to God. As he does this his breathing will become normal, his heart will slow down and he will be free from this attack.'

These words had come, not from my mind, but from a place deep inside me. They had been an interruption from heaven. I followed these instructions and watched. I had one hand on his head and one on his chest, and as I prayed he was filled with the Holy Spirit and he began to speak clearly in an unknown, heavenly tongue. As he did, his heart came back to a normal rhythm and speed, and his breathing was restored. I could feel it happening, the attack was over; he was healed, and was totally amazed and thrilled.

I sent someone to get a drink. A coca-cola was the only thing they could find and as he gulped it down 'I found myself' saying to him, 'If it ever happens again, you'll know what to do.'

Immediately the Holy Spirit said to me, very authoritatively, 'It will never happen again. Tell him, 'It will never happen again.'

I felt very foolish as I explained how the Holy Spirit had just checked me and how those first words were my words, but the voice of God to him was 'It will never happen again.' I know it will never happen again. I know, because I heard from heaven and spoke out what God said.

Learn the lesson

So let me go back over this incident and pull out the lessons I needed to learn:

- I'm simply an instrument for God to use.
- I have no power of my own, I cannot heal.
- God alone has that ability and will do His work in His own way.
- I had been trying to do my 'religious' thing, my 'charismatic' thing, the formula that says, 'In the Name of Jesus, be healed, rise up and walk'. That's perfectly acceptable, good and right, if it's your instruction from

the Holy Spirit, but if it isn't, you're using a formula or what you've read about, or seen others do.

- I had gone into action without listening to heaven.

- I had argued when I was told what to do.

- God had His perfect way for this child to be released.

- When I followed His instructions, he was healed.

- God's direction was 'Tell him what's going to happen.' God had directed Ezekiel to prophesy to the dry bones before anything had happened. (See Ezekiel chapter 37.) I had to say to him, 'This is what is going to happen. I will lay my hands on your head, you will begin to speak in tongues, your breathing will become normal, your heart will slow down.' I was prophesying what was going to happen. Isaiah 44:24–26 says, *'I am the Lord ... who carries out the words of his servants and fulfils the predictions of his messengers.'*

- Don't add human wisdom or dilute what God says. You see that's what I did. I said, 'If this happens again.' God hadn't said that, that was me, that was human wisdom, and I had to repent.

- If I am speaking forth the word of God with His authority, under His direction, then it will come to pass, as surely as God said, *'Let there be light and there was light.'*

- Jeremiah chapter 23:28–29 says, *'... but let the one who has my word speak it faithfully ... Is not my word like fire ... and like a hammer that breaks a rock in pieces?'*

Exodus 4:10–16 recounts how Moses felt so extremely inadequate and how God had to say to him:

'Who gave man his mouth? Who makes him deaf or mute? Who gives him sight or makes him blind? Is it not I, the LORD? Now go; I will help you speak and will teach you what to say.'

(Exodus 4:11–12)

Even then Moses said,

'"O LORD, please send someone else to do it." Then the LORD's anger burned against Moses.' (Exodus 4:13–14)

Eventually God said,

'You shall speak to him [Aaron] *and put words in his mouth; I will help both of you speak and will teach you what to do. He will speak to the people for you, and it will be as if he were your mouth and as if you were God to him.'*

(Exodus 4:15–16)

We are God's servants and He wants us to speak out as if we were His mouth.

Repent of everything that you have done in the past on your own initiative. It might have had the right heart motivation and great compassion, but as the old hymn writer put it,

'The arm of flesh will fail you.
You dare not trust your own.'

(Onward Christian Soldiers)

James 1:19 says:

'My dear brothers, take note of this: Everyone should be quick to listen, slow to speak ...'

Jesus said in John 12:49:

'For I did not speak on my own accord, but the Father who sent me commanded me what to say and how to say it.'

Important points

- Every time we act for God we must first hear from heaven.
- God's words are living and active and will have lasting results.
- Once we have heard from God we can speak and act with boldness and confidence.
- God forgives our mistakes.

Chapter 7

Divine Appointments

As a young Christian I longed to have the confidence to witness to others about Jesus. I had always admired people who were not afraid to speak about salvation, about Jesus, about sin, heaven and hell. It sounded so real and simple when they did it. They loved to lead people to Christ at the end of meetings, but I was always afraid that I would complicate the whole thing and might be responsible for keeping a soul out of heaven. I didn't feel happy with a 'set' routine. Oh yes, I learned the key texts from Romans, I could quote the verses such as, *'The wages of sin is death, but the gift of God is eternal life'*. I could recite the salvation promises, but somehow I always felt awkward, sounding more like a parrot than a real person.

That is until I was baptised in the Holy Spirit, when God set me free from this fear. Suddenly I received the power and resources to be a witness to the things that were so real to me. The first opportunity I had to test this new freedom came when God directed me to speak to a lady on an Irish ferryboat. I did, and what began with a discussion about healing opened into a wonderfully real conversation that eventually led to her receiving Jesus into her life. You can read about that in detail in my first book, *Can You Hear God?*

This first encounter became a prototype, simply to follow instructions given by God, and which now has become my familiar pattern.

I love divine appointments; God makes the connection, you speak out what He is saying to you, the person is ready to hear, it's supernatural, everyone is happy, and it can happen at any moment.

I personally don't feel comfortable with what I call 'cold contact evangelism'. I know many people who love to stand on the street, preach, hand out tracts, pray for the sick, etc. I have also done it, but on each occasion I have tried, I have felt wooden and unnatural.

God has given me a way with which I am familiar and happy. I no longer feel guilty, I now simply say 'God where do You want me to go today? What do You want to me to say?'

A visit to the cemetery

In 1998 our Church held a Tent Mission in the park, mainly focused on evening meetings. During the day teams of people would go out into the town, giving out invitations, witnessing, praying for the sick, preaching and being involved in street drama. The day would begin with prayer, and then we would 'hit the town'. As we spilled out of the prayer room, I joined the crowd heading for the town centre, quite prepared to join in the action. However, as I was walking purposefully down the street God broke into my thoughts and spoke to me, 'Go to the churchyard.'

'What? I don't even know where the churchyard is.' I answered back, but reluctantly headed towards the nearest church, which looked as if it should have a churchyard – but there was none.

'I must have got it wrong, this church has no churchyard.'

But the Holy Spirit was insistent, 'Then ask someone.'

'Oh, they'll think I'm stupid,' I thought, but knew by now that God was on my case, and I needed to obey.

'Where is the nearest churchyard?' I asked a passer-by.

'By the sea front.'

It was more than half a mile away, and as I obediently walked towards the seafront, I asked, 'Why am I going there? It seems a long way to go.'

'You'll meet a man sitting on a bench with a lot of questions that he needs answering,' came the reply.

Doubts flooded my mind as I walked on! 'I'm probably making it up.'

Doubts: 'Why a churchyard?'

Doubts: 'OK, I'll just go in and see. If there's no-one there I will know I got it all wrong.'

When I arrived I saw two benches overlooking the graves. A man was sitting on one of them, while I sat on the empty bench and asked God 'Is that the man?'

'Well, you'll never know if you stay here,' was the reply.

'Oh, help me, Lord.'

'Go and talk to him.'

'Do you mind if I sit on this bench with you?' Nod and silence.

A nudge from the Holy Spirit. 'Go on.'

Tongue-tied. 'Go on.'

So I began, 'You may think this very strange, but God told me to come here this morning and He told me that I would meet a man with questions that needed answering. Are you that man?'

'I think I could be.' The response tumbled out in a thick, Irish accent.

Relax, I love the Irish, I'm a quarter Irish myself.

'Go on, then,' I said to him, 'What do you want to know?'

He replied, 'I'm looking at that grave over there thinking about what happens when you die. Do you know what happens?'

'Yes, I do, I said. I'm a Pastor and I'm a Christian and I can tell you.'

And for one and a half hours we talked and eventually we prayed together. I was thrilled, because it was, just as God said, 'Go to the churchyard, there you will meet a man with many questions that need answering.'

I was so excited by this that two days later I went back to the mission preparation meeting, and again the group were released out onto the streets. This time I asked God the question, 'What do You want me to do today? Do you want me to go back to the churchyard again?'

'No,' the Holy Spirit said, 'Go past the churchyard onto the cliff path.'

And you've guessed it, haven't you? There was the same man, on a different seat, looking at the sea. He saw me before I saw him and you would have thought that I was his best friend.

'You again' he shouted, 'Come and sit down here. Are you real, or are you an angel?'

'Some angel,' I said, and sat down. And again, an hour and a half later with more questions answered – angels were rejoicing – Joyce was rejoicing.

You see, it's so easy when God is at work.

That is how life is meant to be,

free,

fun,

joyful,

exciting,

and

exhilarating.

Unforced rhythms of grace

'Are you tired, worn out, burned out on religion? Come to Me, get away with Me and you'll recover your life. I'll show you

> *how to take a real rest. Walk with me, work with me, watch how I do it. Learn the unforced rhythms of grace. I won't lay anything heavy or ill-fitting on you. Keep company with me and you'll learn to live freely and lightly.'*
>
> (Matthew 11:28–29, *The Message*)

This is what I want for all God's people and myself. 'I'll show you,' Jesus says, 'the unforced rhythms of grace.' That's how Jesus lived. Read the Gospels asking yourself, 'What was Jesus hearing and responding to?'

Put this book down now and pick up your Bible and read John 4:1–42.

Let us see what Jesus did.

- Verse 4: It says, *'He had to go through Samaria.'* Why? Had He heard the Holy Spirit say to him, 'Go through Samaria this time'? 'Had to' has a sense of urgency, doesn't it?
- Verse 6: He was tired and He sat down. He was following the natural rhythms of His body, but I'm sure He was also listening for instructions. 'Am I meant to stop here for a while? Do You want me to sit down now?'
- Verse 7: 'Why is a woman drawing water at noon?' Something funny going on here. Women don't go out in the midday sun to draw water or carry heavy loads in the hottest part of the day. 'Take a second look. Is she happy? What do you see?'
- Verse 8: 'Talk to her. Ask her for a drink.'
- Verse 9: 'Don't get into an argument.'
- Verse 10: 'She really needs living water, see if she takes the bait.'
- Verse 13: 'She does.' 'Tell her about the living water she can get from you.'
- Verse 15: 'She wants the living water, but there is a deeper issue here.'

- Verse 16: 'Ask her about her husband.'
- Verses 17 and 18: 'Tell me what's going on, Father.' A word of knowledge reveals her history. Jesus sees right into her heart, He doesn't condemn her, no judgement.
- Verse 19: God has broken through. 'I can see you are a prophet.'
- Verse 39: 'He told me everything I ever did.' Did He? He didn't actually tell her very much.
- Verse 41: 'Because of His words many believed.'
- Verse 42: *'We no longer believe just because of what you said; now we have heard for ourselves, and we know this man really is the Saviour of the world.'*

There is victory. Lives have been changed. Sorrow has turned to joy. He 'had to' go to Samaria. It was a 'divine appointment'. So what can we learn from this?

Important points

- Be yourself. Don't be a phoney. Don't be limited by the fear of man, but remember that reality communicates reality.
- If you're not yet baptised with the Holy Spirit and fire you've only got to ask. The Father promises to give the Holy Spirit to those who ask (Luke 11:13).
- Ask questions.
  - David did (see 1 Samuel 23:2).
  - Samuel did (see 1 Samuel 16:6).
  - Paul did (see Acts 22:10).
  - The disciples did (see Luke 22:7–13).
- Take a second look – stop and listen. You see God knows everything and everybody and He wants to direct you to meet their needs, to be a giver of living water to them.

Chapter 8

Following a Star!

God can, and will, use any means He chooses in order to communicate with us. We are living in days when God is speaking through His Son's Spirit. Hebrews chapter 1:1–2 says:

> *'In the past God spoke to our forefathers through the prophets at many times and in various ways, but in these last days he has spoken to us by his Son, whom he has appointed heir of all things.'*

At the birth of Jesus, God used a star to guide the wise men. It was something they had studied and believed in, but they still had to choose to move out in obedience and follow it. It would appear that it took time to journey to Jerusalem, and as they travelled they would have had to work through doubts, fears and unbelief, just as I did, as I followed the instructions to go to the churchyard. Would *you* follow a star? Would *you* travel day after day, trusting you were being led to the right place? Or, would you have been saying 'Why is the journey taking so long?' 'Are you sure we should be following that star?' 'Have we got the right one?'

We need to understand that it takes time to learn to trust God. It is a journey of faith. It works both ways; we learn to trust Him and He learns that He can trust us. There is always a risk involved in following the prophetic voice of God; a moment when you can choose to believe what you are hearing, and move into a supernatural dimension, or choose to trust your own logic and stay earthbound. Star followers still find Jesus, but the journey is uncharted. The Wise Men needed persistence to find Jesus, and they journeyed until they did.

In a similar way, the disciples had to learn to trust the details of Jesus' instructions if they were going to accomplish the task He had sent them to do. Jesus was training His disciples as He told them to prepare for the Passover Meal.

Put the book down for a moment and read Luke 22:7–14.

Here the disciples didn't know how or where they were going to accomplish the task, but more detail was given when they asked questions.

- Verse 9: We read, *'"Where do you want us to prepare for it?" they asked.'*
- Verse 10: Jesus replies, *'As you enter the city, a man carrying a jar of water will meet you.'* (Carrying water jars was women's work in those days, and therefore it would not be difficult to pick out a man with a water jar.) ***'Follow him*** *to the house that he enters.'*
- Verses 11–13: *'... **say to** the owner of the house, "The Teacher asks: Where is the guest room, where I may eat the Passover with my disciples?" He will show you a large upper room, all furnished. Make preparations there. They left and found things just as Jesus had told them. So they prepared the Passover.'*

Apply rational thinking and see how doubt could have stopped them being obedient.

- There are many gates to the city of Jerusalem.
- It was not possible for the man to watch every gate.
- What if he starts to question us as we follow him?
- What if the owner of the house is not there?
- What if he replies, 'Who on earth is "the teacher"?'
- What if he sends us away?
- What if there is no guest room?

We don't know how the owner was prepared to comply with all this. It could have been natural. Jesus may have met him and discussed it before. He might have said to Jesus 'If you ever need a room to use, come and ask me.' It could have been a vision, as happened to Cornelius and Peter in Acts chapter 10, where both parties were prepared supernaturally by visions, dreams and angels. Whatever were the facts, the disciples had to trust and obey, and when they did it seemed so easy.

You get another example of this in Mark chapter 11 verses 1–11. Specific instructions are given:

> *'Go to the village ahead of you, and just as you enter it, you will find a colt tied there, which no one has ever ridden. Untie it and bring it here. If anyone asks you, "Why are you doing this?" tell him, "The Lord needs it and will send it back here shortly."'* (Mark 11:2)

They had to go expecting to act according to instructions. Rational thinking asks:

- But what if someone thinks that we're stealing this colt?
- What if we get stopped?

'What if' will always stop you. Trust will cause you to take risks.

They acted in faith and brought the colt to Jesus.

When my daughter Joanna was about eight years old she had warts on her knee. I had tried to treat them with the cream given by the doctor, but they had multiplied and were now covering the whole of her knee. They were very unsightly and we didn't know what else to do.

As I began to pray about it, God said to me 'Speak to those warts and tell them to be removed.' He directed me to Mark 11:22–23 which says:

> *'"Have faith in God," Jesus answered. "I tell you the truth, if anyone says to this mountain, 'Go, throw yourself into the sea,' and does not doubt in his heart but believes that what he says will happen, it will be done for him."'*

Now, I am trained to be a rational thinker; speaking to inanimate objects including warts seemed foolish, but I chose to do what I had been told. I explained to Joanna what I was going to do and then commanded that the warts must go in Jesus' Name. They didn't vanish immediately but began to wither and die. Three days later they appeared to have flattened and one week later they were gone! We were so encouraged, we started to speak to all sorts of minor ailments and saw many healings.

Now I want to jump forward 20 years and tell you another story. My husband and I were ministering to a group of churches in southern Germany. Charles had been teaching from John's gospel, showing how Jesus in His earthly ministry operated in the power of the Holy Spirit, using the gifts of the Spirit. He then asked people to come for prayer, for healing, and to be filled again with the Holy Spirit and to commit themselves to operate in the same way as Jesus.

A lady came forward and said, through tears, 'I want to believe but I cannot, I am so full of doubt and unbelief.' I discovered as I questioned her that she had a small child with impaired hearing. Much prayer had been made for this child but with no tangible result. I talked to her, challenged the unbelief, she repented and turned to go back to her seat. As she was walking away from me, the Holy Spirit spoke to me and said, 'Tell her that when she gets home, she will find her child healed.' I called her back, the words spilled out of my mouth before unbelief had a chance to stop me. My translator asked, 'Have you really said, what I think you've said?'

I repeated, 'Yes, tell her, when she arrives home, her the child will be healed.' I then went on to pray for several other people. It was late and I was ready to return to our lodgings. The mother of this child, however, was still waiting to speak to me. She couldn't believe that what I had said to her could possibly happen. She told me that she had a 40-minute car ride and was very afraid her faith would evaporate on the journey. I established that she could speak in tongues and told her to pray in tongues, out loud, all the way home. I knew that if she obeyed me, she would not have the capacity to drive, pray and reason at the same time. So off she went.

However, I suddenly realised what I had said and was immediately attacked by doubt and fear. What if it was just me? Was it God? Was it arrogance? Was it stupidity? I told Charles what I had said and he encouraged me to keep my faith behind what I had done. I was so tired that I fell asleep as soon as my head hit the pillow. I woke once in the night with more doubt attacks. I told the doubt and fear to leave me but thought, 'They used to stone false prophets!' Then I went back to sleep.

In the morning I got up, prepared for a busy day with several teaching seminars, and went to the meeting. The lady was waiting to greet me as I arrived at the church; she didn't have stones to throw, but was crying with joy and couldn't wait to tell me what had happened.

She had done as I had suggested. She had prayed in tongues during her 40-minute drive. She was still praying when she got home. Her normal practice was to lift the child onto the toilet just before she went to bed and she was still speaking in tongues as she held her child in place. The sleepy, little one said, 'Mummy, will you stop shouting, you're hurting my ears.' The child could hear!

The next morning the child was telling the whole family to be quiet – they were all making far too much noise. A miracle had taken place, hearing had been restored. Hallelujah!

In John chapter 4 one word from heaven was enough to release the woman at the well of Samaria. Scripture says *'The dead will hear the voice of the Son of God and those who hear will live'* (John 5:25). I was absolutely thrilled that as God had spoken, I had been obedient, had spoken out what I heard from heaven, and the result was restored hearing.

Important points

- It takes faith and obedience to follow a star.
- It takes faith and obedience to follow seemingly strange instructions and give specific greetings, as the disciples were told to do.
- It takes faith and obedience to speak to mountains. Your rational mind says 'intelligent people don't do this kind of thing.'
- It takes time to learn to trust God. It's a journey, but you have to start sometime. It has taken me many years to learn faith and trust and I'm still journeying. I want to be quicker in responding to the voice from heaven. Confess your failure to act on what God has said. Deal honestly with your doubts and fears and your disappointments. There are times when we think we've heard the voice of God, acted on it, and we haven't had the results we thought we'd get.

- Decide today to listen to the voice of God's Spirit and to obey. You might fear you'll get it wrong, but you could get it right and see miracles. Isn't it worth the risk?

Chapter 9

A Life-Giving Rebuke

Start this chapter by reading 1 Samuel 2:27 to the end of chapter 3.

Will you say it as it is?

God had revealed a very difficult message to Samuel and He was testing him to see if he would have the courage to 'say it as it is.' Would he repeat it to Eli? Would he try to soften the blow? Who does he fear, God or Eli? It's great to bring words of encouragement, hope and comfort to people, but sometimes we have to bring words of challenge and correction. This is never easy. It takes courage and sensitivity to know what to say and how to say it. Jesus is our example and He did and said only what He heard from the Father. Sometimes He brought harsh words. Remember the Rich Young Ruler? He didn't want to hear the command to sell all and follow Jesus. Peter wasn't very thrilled when he was publicly rebuked, but Jesus wasn't playing 'keep the people happy', He was obeying the Father's voice.

In the scripture you've just read, Samuel was being trained by God to be Israel's prophet. He would have many confrontational things ahead, especially with King Saul. God had to know that He could trust him to be accurate. He had to know whether Samuel would be afraid of men, especially older, more experienced men. Would he give God's message, even when he knew it would cause distress?

God had spoken to Samuel in 1 Samuel chapter 3:11–15 and he was afraid to tell Eli what he had heard. But in 1 Samuel chapter 3 verse 18 it says, *'So Samuel told him everything, hiding nothing from him.'* Samuel didn't know that Eli had already heard this message from another prophet and that when Samuel spoke it, it merely came as a confirmation.

Many times, if you have to bring a difficult, corrective word, God will already have spoken to the person directly or through someone else. What you speak will bring a confirmation that adds weight to the original word. Most times, the person concerned already knows the truth of the matter. Scripture says, *'Every matter must be established by the testimony of two or three witnesses'* (2 Corinthians 13:1).

In 2 Samuel chapter 12, Nathan brought correction to David after his adultery with Bathsheba. As he spoke out the words, *'You are the man!'* David knew he had been found out, received the rebuke and cried out to God, *'I have sinned.'* It isn't easy to speak the truth, especially when you expect a reaction or know that it will hurt. However, God needs to know if we can be trusted and if our fear of God is bigger than our fear of man.

Those who have the responsibility of speaking for God will have to pass this test. I have walked with God for over 50 years and I am shocked at how few Christian leaders will confront in love, or even without love! We need leaders who will follow Paul's charge to Timothy, to preach the word, in season and out of season, who will

> **correct**, **rebuke** and encourage, with patience and careful instructions.

So why won't we do it? Fear of man, intimidation, fear of rejection, sentimental love, wanting to be popular. I thank

God for the very few courageous people who have given me godly rebuke, which I have needed and has brought freedom and life. I know the personal courage they exercised when they did it, and thank God they feared Him more than me.

Proverbs 15:31 says:

> *He who listens to a life-giving rebuke*
> *will be at home among the wise.*

I have a very courageous husband, more afraid of God than man. In his personality he is quiet and has a gentleness which is very strong, but when he has to bring a corrective word, he doesn't shirk that responsibility; he doesn't welcome it, it is never easy, but he will do it as before God, with faith that it will be a life-giving rebuke.

My personality is very different. I can rebuke and be brutally truthful when angry. That is not God, it has often caused hurt and pain, is not life-giving, and can crush and do untold damage. Giving a life-giving rebuke is bringing what God has instructed you to bring with trembling, but because it is necessary, and with faith that it will divide between soul and spirit, joints and marrow and expose the thoughts and intentions of the heart. We cannot in the same situation be both a man-pleaser and a God-pleaser. For those whom God entrusts with this kind of leadership responsibility there is a loneliness, hence Paul's admonition in Hebrews 13:17 to pray for our leaders.

For years I was a man pleaser, I would rather please than offend and I have had some hard lessons to learn. But God will not stop His training because I squeal. He knows what I have to learn, and I don't want to keep going round this mountain. I need to move on. I have needed a lot of healing because I didn't want to be rejected. But God is patient and kind, He wants to use us to speak His word, however difficult, He never gives up; He will have His way with us.

I was taking a conference in Austria and my translator was a young lady from Youth With A Mission. We worked together for a week. and at one point she asked me what I felt about a certain kind of praying. She expressed a concern about certain young women she knew who were convinced that God had shown them who they should marry and who were 'claiming' these young men and thanking God that they would be their future husbands!

I had spoken my mind to her and together we discussed the dangers of this kind of manipulation. On the last day of the conference I was asked to pray with a lady, and I needed a translator. I discovered the lady I was to minister to was convinced that God had told her who she would marry. The man concerned was certainly not interested and, in fact, had asked his pastor to speak to this woman and correct her. She was a strong personality and no one wanted to do it. Everyone involved was fearful of the expected reaction.

I couldn't escape; I think God was amused! I had spoken very strongly to my translator a few days earlier on this very subject and now I had to confront the same issues with this lady, in the presence of my translator.

It's fairly easy to be abstract and very bold, talking about hypothetical situations. But face to face – whoops! It's another matter. I did it but it wasn't easy. The lady didn't like me – and said so. But there was no escape and I believe she needed to hear what God said and felt about the situation. I had compassion for her, but I couldn't soften it. I could only pray that God would bring revelation and free her from this bondage, and that she would see how she was spoiling not only her relationship with this man, but also affecting her whole church, who were so embarrassed, but didn't know how to challenge her.

I learned a lesson. You see, God put me in a situation where I could not compromise what I had already spoken out to this young translator, and that was good for me.

God will keep on confronting us with important issues until we learn the lesson. At this same conference I had another opportunity to test whether I had learned my lesson. I was sharing a meal table with a newly converted Austrian doctor and an older lady who I knew quite well. This lady had been very generous to our family; we had used her skiing lodge for a holiday. The conversation moved to the subject of praying for the dead, and the 'fireworks' began. In the heated argument that ensued, I didn't like the aggressive behaviour of the doctor, even if her doctrine was correct. On the other hand I had no desire to offend my gracious generous friend, so I remained almost silent, and in fact compromised truth. I was in a 'No Win' situation. One party despised me, the other looked for support that I could not give. I felt awful, and left the dining room to do business with God. He reminded me that truth is truth. I don't have to defend it, but I do have to state it. My opinion does not matter, but what God says does. Jesus said many things the crowd didn't like and the religious leaders argued about, but He didn't climb down. He spoke what the Father gave Him and didn't add or take away from it. I repented of cowardice, and fear of man as I realised I had offended this young doctor, compromised God's word and tried to be kinder than God. What a mess. God forgave me, it was harder to forgive myself. Now I had to repair the damage. I sought out the doctor but discovered she had already left the conference, not at all pleased with me. I then asked God for an opportunity to speak with her before leaving the country.

Some days later I was taking a meeting in Vienna. The doctor did not know I would be speaking, but she was in the congregation. Her face told me everything. There was no way she could receive God's word from me. At the end of the meeting I moved quickly to catch her before she left. We were able to talk honestly. She acknowledged her aggression, and I my fear of man. I apologised for not supporting her and in doing so compromising truth. I learned a big lesson; my opinions count for nothing, what God says is truth and must not be altered or compromised. I do not need to justify what He says or defend it. Truth might offend, it does divide, but I must always bend to it and not deny it. What an amazing combination was found in Jesus – full of grace and truth.

Important points

- *'Fear of man will prove to be a snare, but whoever trusts in the LORD is kept safe'* (Proverbs 29:25). Very few of us enjoy confrontation, but you may have to give a rebuke or a straight word to someone. Can God trust you to do it?
- A very helpful book on this subject is *Breaking Intimidation* by John Bevere. You may well have been intimidated in the past and need to release yourself from those situations, so God can take you forward and train you to be a Samuel, prepared to bring His word however difficult.
- If you have failed in this area, repent and ask God to show you why. What are you afraid of? Please deal with it. It could mean life and death to someone in the future.
- If you are a parent or have responsibility with children, ask God for His ability to correct positively. He always gives a way; He always encourages us that we can do what He asks and He will help us. We're not on our own.

Chapter 10

What About Practical Things?

God is just as committed to the practical issues of our lives as the spiritual ones. The Holy Spirit will come alongside us to help us in every area of life, if we will be prepared to seek His help.

The missing lens

I was carrying my 3-year-old son from our house to the main conference centre where we worked. It was a dark night, raining and blowing a gale. I stumbled; Ben grabbed me and knocked the contact lens out of my eye. I had no idea where it had dropped, nor could I stay and search in the rain.

Consequently, I arrived for evening prayers very, very upset, and it showed. Someone asked me what was the matter, and I poured out my misery and frustration.

Then came the usual questions: 'Have you forgiven him?'

I was pretty mad, to be honest. But I knew what I must do.

'Yes, I forgive him. But that doesn't change the situation, does it?'

'Let's pray,' they said. To me it was so super-spiritual.

Outwardly I complied, but inwardly I was making 'phone

calls to my optician for a replacement lens and was working out the quickest way that I could get it.

They were still praying, when a 'word of knowledge' came from the Lord indicating that the missing lens would be found 'near the dog dirt.'

Giggles came from some of the kids; unbelief and cynicism from me.

'Let's get a car out, beam a headlight down the driveway and see if we can find it.'

I tried to be as enthusiastic as possible, but inside me I thought, 'What a crazy lot you are. It's wet, windy and dark. This is a waste of time. Why on earth don't you stay warm and let me send for my replacement lens?'

They searched, but there was no success. I was confirmed in my scepticism and unbelief.

The next morning I promptly made the 'phone call ordering my replacement lens, but I was also receiving lots of 'phone calls from the rest of the community encouraging me to believe the word of knowledge!

But God – and Marigold!

Later that day, I was returning home after a walk in the woods with my children, and as we entered the house there was a shriek, 'Look Mum, there's a matchbox on the table and a note from Marigold.' Inside the box was a contact lens, whole, unscratched; and an explanation. My friend, Marigold, had not despised the prophetic word, as I had. She had received it, believed it and acted on it. She walked the 100 yards of tarmac drive looking for dog dirt. She found it, and beside it floating in a pool of rain between the dips in the tarmac, was my lens. Nobody had walked on it because it was so near the dog dirt! Her faith was rewarded. I rejoiced, but was quick to ask God's forgiveness and repent as I cancelled my lens replacement order.

Much chastened, I put my cleaned contact lens back in my eye with a 'Thank you, Jesus' pouring out of my heart. God has all knowledge and all wisdom; nothing is hidden from Him. Isn't it reasonable for God to reveal what He knows? Why does it surprise us?

In search of donkeys

It was like looking for a needle in a haystack, only it was donkeys in the hills of Ephraim, Benjamin and Zuph! Saul and his servant had spent three days searching, and there was still no sign of the missing animals. They were sore, sweaty and wanted to go home. Saul was about to give up the search, realising by this time his father would be more anxious about him than the beasts. The servant was also giving up searching, but for a different reason. He remembered that in this geographical region there lived a man of God, highly respected, and with the reputation that all his words come true. He suggested to Saul that this seer might help them find their elusive quarry.

God also wanted Saul and Samuel to meet for different and infinitely more far-reaching purposes. Samuel, who travelled around Israel visiting north, south, east and west on a regular basis 'happened' to be in that place at that particular time. They met and he was able to tell Saul, *'As for the donkeys you lost three days ago, do not worry about them; they have been found.'* (Details of this divine encounter are found in 1 Samuel chapters 9 and 10.)

The coin in the fish

When Jesus was here on earth, those in authority were constantly seeking to trip Him up. On one occasion they asked Peter, *'Does your teacher pay temple tax?'* He was quick to reply, *'Yes, he does.'* However, it would seem that the tax had not been paid, and it appeared that Judas, the treasurer, was not around. The pressure was on. Jesus was committed to live righteously. Now they were looking to Him to pay the tax right there and then, and they had no money. But God had. Jesus now looked to His Father to hear from Him how this dilemma might be resolved. Peter knew how to catch fish, for he was a fisherman, and God was fully aware of that natural talent and quite happy to put it to good use. God also knew that there was a fish out there with a coin in its mouth. This was revealed to Jesus and He sent Peter to catch the fish. Out popped the four-drachma coin, the tax was paid, and the plot to humiliate Jesus had been foiled. This species of fish are still caught in the Sea of Galilee today, and they are often found to have coins in their mouths. In fact when I visited Israel, I ate one. It was delicious! (You can read this incident in Matthew 17:24–27.)

A gut feeling

Our youngest son Ben is an aircraft engineer working with Mission Aviation Fellowship in Tanzania. He told me he had a 'gut feeling' he would find a major fault on the aircraft that had just arrived for servicing. He felt compelled not only to overhaul the engine as required, but to check the airframe in a much more thorough way than normal. He was like a detective searching for an invisible clue, which he eventually found. It was corrosion in a part of the landing gear, which could have been life threatening. He had heard God. Take your gut feelings to God and ask for more information.

Think of a number

My son, Craig, had so many gifts to take back to Bulgaria, after a recent trip to England, that he needed an extra suitcase. We remembered that we had one up in the attic, which many years ago had been left behind by our daughter. It was found, but it had a combination lock on it and we couldn't open it, nor could we make contact with her to get the necessary information. So we were now trying to fiddle with the dials, racing against time. Perhaps we would hit on the right combination just by chance.

I said, 'Why don't we ask the Lord to tell us the combination?'

The response I had was not very positive; I could feel the vibes, 'Oh don't get all holy on us, Mum.'

But I prayed and said, 'Try 6356.'

Again, the facial expressions and retorts said it all, 'You're not serious, are you?'

But to Craig's credit, he turned the dials and ping, the case opened. Hallelujah!

The next comment was full of unbelief, something like, 'Well, it was probably a fluke.'

But it wasn't, it was the answer to a need by an all-seeing, all-knowing, loving Father. We were thankful and joyful and the soon the presents were winging their way to Bulgaria. But so many times we don't ask for God's help and when He does act we would rather explain it away, crediting what He does to chance, or something else.

By the way, I'm not planning on doing the lottery!

The Bible says, *'You do not have because you do not ask'* (James 4:3, NKJV).

Climbing incidents

It was Christmastime and we were staying in a cottage at Land's End. The proposal for the day was that I drop the boys and Charles at a given spot where they were to spend the day rock climbing, whilst we girls went shopping in Penzance. I was to meet them at 4 o'clock at the same place where I had left them. The girls were dropped back at the cottage and I proceeded to the cliffs, parked the car and began to walk to the pick up point.

No boys
no sign of any boys
light fading
sea roaring
wind blowing
fear rising
steps quickening
no boys.

I waited for 30 minutes, stewing, all the time trying to work out what I should do. I prayed for safety, I mentally called out the coast guard, used the topography to mark the position on the cliff so that they could be reached. At no time did I ask the Lord 'Where are they?' Eventually I left and walked back to the car. On the way I met a man with a dog and said, 'I'm looking for two teenage boys with their father. They were dressed for rock climbing. Have you seen them?' He suggested I enquire at a nearby cottage and so I knocked on the door and asked the same question.

'Yes, they left a message here that they had decided to climb at Zennor instead. You need to pick them up there.'

It's amazing how quickly fear can change to anger. We rendezvoused; they were alive and well. I, however, was not only cross with them for their lack of clear instructions on how to find them, I was very upset and disappointed with myself. 'Why hadn't I asked God? Why hadn't I asked the simple question 'Are they safe, do I need to be anxious? Is there something You can tell me, guide me, direct me?' But I had asked none of these things. I had been very near to panicking.

Six months later I was again involved in a climbing incident, this time in Scotland on the mountains between Lochcarron and Applecross. The boys had been out all day and we had arranged to meet them before the light went, but again no boys. This time I had learned my lesson and asked the right question. I heard the Holy Spirit saying, 'It's taken a lot longer than they thought to accomplish this climb, but they're safe but very tired. They'll be here in about an hour. Don't fret, don't shout at them when they arrive, relax and wait, they'll come.' I have to say that even with that assurance I couldn't sit still and read a book. I used the binoculars and saw two, fly-sized climbers descending a rock face, very tired and eventually they became visible as our two sons, and all was well.

Some of you may still be thinking, 'Is God really that interested in the petty details of my life?' Yes He is!

Important points

- God is interested in every detail of your life.
- God knows where things are and when people are in danger, and he will tell you if you ask.
- This is all about developing a relationship and trust. Repent over the times you have belittled other people's faith and testimony and called God's intervention 'chance' or 'luck'.
- Ask God to teach you to seek His help in every detail of life. Many people start with parking spaces. God knows where they are at any given time, so try asking instead of fuming!

Chapter 11

Children Can Be Sensitive to God's Spirit

Jesus valued children. He understood that their spirits are very receptive to truth and they often have as much understanding as adults. One day He took a little child as an example. It's recorded in Matthew 18:3–5:

> *'I tell you the truth, unless you change and become like little children, you will never enter the kingdom of heaven. Therefore, whoever humbles himself like this child is the greatest in the kingdom of heaven. And whoever welcomes a little child like this in my name welcomes me.'*

We are challenged to become child-like, not childish. Trusting, unpretentious, not self-conscious, not contaminated by unbelief, pure in heart, and not afraid to fail.

Children are also receptive to new truth, ready to experiment. We see this in Matthew 11:25:

> *'At this time Jesus said, "I praise you, Father, Lord of heaven and earth, because you have hidden these things from the wise and learned, and revealed them to little children. Yes, Father, for this was your good pleasure.'*

Matthew 5:8 says, *'Blessed are the pure in heart, for they will see God.'* I am convinced that children can see God in a simpler and easier way than adults.

In the Old Testament God commanded the Israelites, through Moses, to talk to their children about God all the time. In Deuteronomy 6:5–9 it says:

> *'Love the LORD your God with all your heart and with all your soul and with all your strength. These commandments that I give you today are to be upon your hearts. Impress them on your children. Talk about them when you sit at home and when you walk along the road, when you lie down and when you get up. Tie them as symbols on your hands and bind them on your foreheads. Write them on the doorframe of your houses and on your gates.'*

If God is real to you, that reality will communicate to your children. It is important that we lead our children to living faith. It doesn't just happen. They need to know that they have been born again, are forgiven and have the life of Jesus within. Once our children know Jesus, we can teach them that God wants to talk to them and wants them to talk to Him. We need to encourage them. God has no grand-children. My children are my brothers and sisters in the family of God and I need to respect them. Woe to me if I cause them to stumble in their relationship with God. If you create the expectancy in them that they can hear God's voice, they will.

Jumping up and down

When my son Daniel was aged seven, Trevor Dearing, an early pioneer in the move of the Holy Spirit, was with us for a weekend of ministry. Trevor's healing and deliverance ministry was accompanied by signs and wonders. As he prayed with people they often fell down under the power of God's Holy Spirit, a very unusual phenomenon in those days. As we always talked about everything at home, as we are commanded in Deuteronomy, Daniel was well aware that these things were happening in the meetings. He was fascinated and wanted to go and see the people fall down!

We were not in the habit of taking our smaller children to evening meetings. It was the era of bed at 6 pm and hopefully not being seen or heard until dawn at least. Daniel was very enthusiastic, but I talked with Trevor as I knew my young son was only wanting to see the manifestations. Trevor felt that he should come and he did. He sat on the front row, sang loudly all the songs he knew, listened a bit to the message, not much, but as soon as the ministry began he wanted to know everything. Then to my great surprise he slipped my clutches and marched out for prayer. Trevor caught my eye and I indicated 'Pray for him.' I thought, 'this is outside my control.' Hands were laid on Daniel, he didn't fall over, but was quiet and sat unusually still for the rest of the meeting.

The next day I heard him recounting the whole incident to his brother, Craig, and I have to confess, I listened outside their bedroom door. He was telling Craig about the people who were falling over, and that some were speaking in a strange language. Craig then said, 'What did it sound like?' Daniel, who had started to jump up and down on his bed, began what he thought was mimicking speaking in tongues. He thought he was making it up, that it was just gobbledygook. Craig was laughing and Daniel was enjoying the fun. But outside the door, I was amazed as I listened to a beautiful supernatural tongue.

I walked into the bedroom and they both started giggling and Craig said, 'Daniel's pretending to speak in tongues.'

'He isn't pretending,' I said. 'You might think you're making it up, Daniel, but you're not. You're speaking in a heavenly language.'

God had honoured that step of faith and filled Daniel with His Holy Spirit. He never looked back, he would lie in bed at night and pray in tongues. 'It is easier than praying in English,' he would often say!

It wasn't long before Craig and Joanna wanted to know more, and we prayed for each of our children to be filled with God's Holy Spirit and begin an adventure with Him. Each of them was under the age of ten when they received the Holy Spirit. It didn't turn them into angels. They were normal, growing, developing children, but they were all aware of a supernatural God, who had chosen to communicate with them, and through them, if they would let Him. The spiritual, unseen realm was real.

We encouraged them, shared our own experiences with them, told them of things that we read which they would understand, accounts of healings, miracles and revivals. We encouraged them to pray for others. Sometimes they weren't at all receptive and could appear to be totally disinterested. But God, who had begun a good work, had put in them an expectancy of knowing Him and hearing Him, which kept developing as the years went on.

Helping Dad

Joanna, our elder daughter, is very sensitive to God's Spirit; sees pictures and often has words of encouragement to give to others. Charles took her on a ministry trip to Hungary, and at one of the meetings Charles was asked to pray for about 30 pastors and speak prophetic words into their lives. He told Joanna to listen for words from God for these men and women. She stood in front of one of these men and described an amazing picture of a garden full of weeds, which need tending. The group gasped as God spoke through a totally innocent sixteen year old, who knew nothing about this man. She was describing the neglect and she gave him God's instructions to bring order back into his life.

No one else could have spoken so plainly, so innocently and sweetly, and he received the corrective word that he needed. Everyone else knew he needed it, but didn't know how to tell him. This man was out of touch with God, a black sheep, and God chose this very pure instrument, who had clearly received this word straight from heaven.

Moving house

Another time, as a family, we were seeking God concerning our future. He had spoken to us about leaving Kingdom Faith Ministries and beginning a new season in our lives. We were not clear where we should base ourselves as a family and we were pursuing a couple of options. One night we had a power cut and in the dark, huddling around a gas fire for warmth, Coralie, then fifteen, asked 'Would you like to hear what God has been telling me about this situation?' She returned from her bedroom with a notebook and began to read what God had said; it was exactly what we needed to hear and we received it as confirmation of God's direction. This was amazing because at this time Coralie was not very communicative; we hadn't really realised that she was listening to God, and so for us it was a great source of encouragement, not only that she had heard God, but that she was seeking to hear Him on a regular basis.

I asked her, 'When did you start listening like this?' She told me that about a year before when one of her youth group had laid hands on her and said, 'God is going to give you sensitive ears.' That expectancy caused Coralie to buy a notebook and start listening.

Craig forced me into interpreting tongues. He was speaking in tongues one day and then said, 'Tell me what I am saying please, Mum.' So I very quickly asked God to enable me to interpret his tongue and surprised myself as I did so.

Born again

Ben gave his heart to Jesus as a five year old, and it happened in a very unusual way. One night, as I was putting him to bed and was encouraging him to pray for his brothers and sisters, he totally refused to pray for Craig and Daniel. This was surprising, as he always wanted to do things with his two older brothers, 'the big boys'. They were on a half-term holiday and had decided to go for a long walk, which included walking around the lake in the grounds of the Hyde estate where we lived, followed by a four mile trek through the woods. They didn't want to be slowed down by a five year old as they knew they would end up carrying him most of the way. So when they found him following them they told him to go home. He didn't and kept trailing them until they reached the lake; they then threatened him by holding him over the water by his dungaree straps and said, 'Go home or we will drop you in.'

Naturally, he became very frightened and they ended up making him walk the whole way. So one very unhappy, unforgiving, little boy was not going to pray for Craig and Daniel. Oh no! Certainly not! Then to my surprise he began to cry and say he wanted his name written in God's book, he wanted to be Jesus' friend and wanted Jesus to come and live in his heart. I couldn't think where he had heard about this. Then I remembered that, three weeks previously he had been in a meeting when Colin Urquhart had been speaking about having our names written in the Lamb's Book of Life. I remembered that at that time Ben was making a nuisance of himself with a toy car, brrumming it up and down. I had been constantly telling him to sit still and be quiet; I had no idea he was taking in so much but now I was able to pray for him.

He forgave his brothers and admitted that he had been a pest; and just when I thought peace had been restored, there were more tears and he said, 'It hasn't worked.' 'What hasn't worked?' 'Well, I can't say things like Craig and Daniel.' Light dawned. He wanted to be able to pray in tongues. So we prayed some more and asked Father God to fill him with the Holy Spirit. He did and Ben got his new language.

At that time he had not started primary school and was attending a pre-school run by some mothers and some of the young ladies who were part of the community at the Hyde. Several days later one of these young women, who I knew, asked me 'What's happened to Ben? It's like having a different child in the Playgroup. He's so much easier and he's just different.' He was; he had become a child of the living God.

Important points

- Talk often about spiritual things, talk about answers to prayer, about what you are hearing, about what you are asking and believing for, about what you are reading. If you read something faith building will you share it with your family?
- Will you recognise that children can enter into spiritual reality very easily? There is no limit to the age when God begins to reveal Himself.
- Will you repent if you have limited God in your thinking?
- Will you recognise that within a family all children are different, both in their appetite for God and the time when He starts to awaken them? Be sensitive, don't force the pace. They are God's precious children and we are guardians and trainers for a season.
- Will you be an encourager? Will you create expectancy? Will you give opportunities for experience and believe your children will grow spiritually, as fast, or even faster than you?

Chapter 12

Training the Next Generation

We have five children who are all fully committed to following Jesus, married to Christians, and are seeking to train their own children to walk in the Spirit. Reality will communicate reality, and as they seek as families to live before God in an open and transparent way, God will reveal Himself. Children will hear from God in a way that is best suited to their age and understanding. Never despise what a child is hearing from God. Sometimes it will be their imagination, but as you encourage and listen to them, you will help them to grow in confidence and sensitivity.

There is the desire in parents to see our children advance beyond us in every area of life, mentally, emotionally, physically and spiritually. We do not want them to repeat our mistakes and weaknesses, but to develop without our emotional scars. In areas where we have experienced lack, we want them to have prosperity. This is godly generational thinking. We are living in the '**me**' generation with all its shrivelled perspectives, but the Bible speaks of the God of Abraham, Isaac and Jacob.

We want each succeeding generation to advance on all fronts. It is relatively easy to see this happening on the material side, but we need equal commitment to see it happen spiritually.

In Ghana I met Elder Atta, a hard-working taxi driver, who has dedicated his life to provide university education for his children, which he had been denied because of poverty. I saw such joy on his face as he told me of Emmanuel studying in England, Esther in her final year at Kumasi University and Lydia about to study medicine, but he was equally committed to their spiritual growth. His thinking is generational.

Parenting is hard work; there are disappointments as well as encouragements. It's a roller coaster ride, and we need constantly to keep our focus on God's promises, especially when we are in the 'war zone'. Fear will shout loudly emphasising our failure, mocking our hopes. Don't give up! God desires – and will have – another generation who know and walk with Him.

Your children have amazing spiritual potential, which I encourage you to recognise and develop, and I want to dispel the myth that God is only willing to communicate with adults.

I want to see Jesus

Our eldest grandchild, Gillian, was three years old when she told her mother, Milena, that she wanted to see Jesus. Milena did not ridicule this simple and charming request, but gave her clear and helpful instructions, 'Tell Jesus you want to see Him, close your eyes, keep them shut and you will see Him.' Gillian sat still for a very long time and when she opened her eyes she spoke out what she had seen.

'Jesus came and picked me up. He had a packet of "Smarties" in His hand and He was very kind.'

That was it. She didn't describe His face, nothing was added, but there was no doubt that she had experienced

Jesus' love in a way that she could receive. We thought the 'Smarties' were wonderful!

At six years old, Gillian had been very difficult and disobedient, and had been sent to her bedroom to think about her actions. As she sat quietly in her room, the Holy Spirit began to speak to her and said, 'You were wrong and you need to go and apologise to your mum and ask for forgiveness.'

As she returned to the family room she did just that, which may not seem remarkable to you, but at the time Gillian was going through that very difficult stage when she seldom admitted to being wrong about anything. She also was having great difficulty in saying sorry or asking for forgiveness.

When God speaks to a six year old, it is certainly more powerful than the nagging of frustrated parents!

A word about apologies

I often hear children and adults, when being asked to apologise for some misdemeanour, simply shouting a 'Sorry' as they walk out of the room, to which the expected response is 'Oh, that's all right.' Peace may be restored, but forgiveness has not been sought or received. It is important that repentance is specific, and we have trained our children to say, 'Please forgive me for . . . ' specifying what they had done, to which our response will be, 'I forgive you.' This is what the Bible teaches about forgiveness.

That's our house

Craig and Milena and their family are now living in Bulgaria. When they first arrived they moved in with Milena's family, but it was soon obvious they needed a home of their own. They had attempted to rent a house nearby, but the owner had rebuffed all approaches. However, every time they walked past the house Gillian spoke out, 'We are going to live in that house. I've asked Jesus and He says that's our house.' Gillian was so insistent that Craig plucked up courage once again to speak to the landlord, in obedience to this word from Gillian. He was amazed to find a complete change of heart and attitude, and within days they had moved in.

'Smiley Week'

Gillian came over from Bulgaria last summer to stay for three weeks. One of the purposes was to attend a children's holiday week in Devon called 'Smiley Week'. Some time before she had asked God a question and during this week He answered it in a vision.

In the vision Gillian was walking through a garden, at the end of which was an extremely beautiful golden castle. She entered the castle walking on a purple and golden rug, opened a door and there in front of her were two staircases. She chose the left one and followed it upstairs, past a distinctive purple shell on a stand. She then approached a golden stand with a book on it, and as she reached out to pick up the book it started to grow and felt very warm in her hands. The vision faded and the second part came the next day.

Again, she was holding the book, but couldn't open it. She looked and saw that next to it was another stand with a key that was glowing. As she picked up the key, it grew in her hand and became the right size to open the book. The book was a Bible and the key opened it to John 14:18 and Gillian read the words *'I will not leave you as orphans; I will come to you.'* She might have heard that verse before, or might have read it herself, but she would not have been able to know where to find it. Those words answered her question and released a new assurance of God's love for her. It also thrilled her because of the beauty she had seen and the wonder of the castle. She saw it as the place where God lived and where she was welcome.

When she returned to our home, Gillian was so excited by this vision, she recounted it in great detail, and I encouraged her to write it down before it was forgotten. It is a good practice to encourage your children to get journals and to write down words and visions or draw pictures and keep them, because it is very easy to forget what God says.

Jesus makes all the difference

When Campbell, my oldest grandson, was seven years old he heard a testimony from a girl at 'SuperChurch,' our children's church, telling how she had invited Jesus into her heart. This greatly impressed him and he went home and told his mum that he too wanted Jesus in his heart. Later that night, Tanya explained what it meant in detail to receive Jesus and prayed for him.

A remarkable change took place in Campbell. His strops and stubbornness had not only affected the family, but also caused real problems at school. From the time Jesus came into his heart, there was a dramatic change, the moods became less frequent and he would get back into his sunny self much more quickly with Jesus' help. Perfection had not arrived, but knowing Jesus had made a real difference!

Some time later Daniel and Tanya took their children to a 24-7 Prayer Vigil. During their hour in the Prayer Room, Campbell heard people praying in tongues. He said he'd like to be able to do this, and as they prayed, Campbell asked God to fill him with His Holy Spirit and God gave him a new prayer language. He had just a few words to start with, which he used, but he is now growing in confidence.

Around this time he was struggling with school, and again God spoke to him and said, 'Be baptised.' God told him that as he was obedient He would help him at school. This was so real that Campbell literally pestered his grandpa every time they met. 'When can I be baptised?' It took a while for us to realise that this was very important to him and it wasn't just a childish whim.

In Living Waters Church we teach our children about spiritual gifts and they are encouraged to use them. Recently Campbell was able to give a word of knowledge to an older lady that both surprised and helped her.

Children are very different in the way they hear from God, Gillian often sees pictures and visions, Campbell is more down to earth and practical in what he sees. Ella, his sister, was quite happy to tell me 'Campbell hears God a lot. I don't.' It is not a problem or an issue, and she recently told her mum, 'When I lie in bed I know Jesus holds my hand. I'm fine. I'm quite happy.' That's Ella!

God knows the intimate details

I was recently speaking to a lady who told me that as a child she had been very lonely, not able to talk to her mother about personal, intimate things. As she awoke one day, she heard a voice inside her say, 'Something will happen to you today. But it's OK, you're not to be worried or to be afraid.' She went off to school and during the day went to the bathroom and discovered that her first period had started. She had not been prepared for this either mentally or emotionally, but her Heavenly Father was watching and He cared for her, His assurance had averted fear.

Supernatural warnings

Anna's conception had been announced by an angel, at a time when her mother Faith didn't know whether she would ever have any more children. Edmond and Faith, from Burundi, were at a Bible College in England when one night

Faith was awoken by the Holy Spirit and told to go to the College Chapel. There an angel told her that she would have a baby girl, who was to be called Anna, and that she would be a prophetess and be a great blessing to them as a couple and to Burundi as a nation. Children conceived miraculously often have a prophetic dimension in their lives.

Faith became pregnant almost immediately, bought pink baby clothes which she took back to Burundi, and told everybody she was having a girl. In due time Anna was born and brought great joy to all the family. She was a placid, easy child, always compliant. However, one Sunday morning when about 18 months old, she suddenly seemed to have changed; she would do nothing that the family wanted. She was not yet talking, but she seemed disturbed and wouldn't let them dress her, then refused her breakfast, wouldn't walk and didn't want to get into the car seat. What was going on? She seemed intent on keeping her parents from getting to church on time.

Eventually, very late, they managed to get everyone into the car and drive to the Eglise Vivant at Jabe where their church met. Her delaying tactics saved their lives. A terrorist bomb had exploded at the road junction close to the church and killed a number of people. The explosion had happened at exactly the time they would have expected to arrive at church. The devil meant it for them, the future leaders of African Revival Ministries, and God used this baby to prevent them from being at that road junction at the time of the blast. It became quite clear that her unusual behaviour had in fact been quite deliberate.

When Anna could talk, on several occasions she said to her father, 'Don't go down that road today.' They heeded her warning and by doing so avoided similar life threatening incidents.

Elliot is a young boy in our church who has visions and his mother Sarah encourages him to draw what he sees. At one time he was in bed and had a vision of a cobra coming towards him from the corner of the room; it lunged at him and bit him, but he didn't feel anything and God told him that the snake was the devil but he couldn't hurt him. The next day, while in a supermarket, they met a clown who made Elliott a snake out of balloons and as it was given to him, he heard God say, 'Nothing will in any way harm you.' What a great revelation to have as a nine year old.

Another time he found himself fascinated as he looked out at a special sunset. The light was spectacular and he took a photograph. He heard the Holy Spirit say, 'Nothing is as beautiful as My glory.' God was creating an expectancy and a desire in this young child for more of Himself.

I know of another child who would hide every time a certain person came into the house. Later the parents realised that the child had perceived danger and a wrong spirit, and the child was later proved to be right.

I don't want to give the wrong impression about my children or grandchildren. They are quite normal and act as all children do. They need plenty of strong discipline. They are capable of being rude, arrogant and selfish. My observation is that God isn't waiting for perfection before He shows His love and desire to communicate. It is exactly the same with us as adults who have, perhaps, learned more self-control but still need to be changed into His likeness.

Your children need every tool that the Holy Spirit can give them and, most certainly, His power for daily living. Schools are not neutral territory. Your children are on the front line, probably more so than you. Pray. Listen to them, really listen. Remember that they are not only your children, they are God's children and your brothers and sisters in Christ.

Note: I have used my older grandchildren as examples, with their permission. I have been challenged as I have asked them to tell me about their experiences. I have tried to listen and share my excitement, and encourage them. They are still children, their character needs to develop, but they are growing up with a God awareness. Proverbs 22:6 says:

> *'Train a child in the way he should go,*
> *and when he is old he will not turn from it.'*

Important points

- A child's spirit is ageless and is sensitive to spiritual things.
- Never belittle what young children tell you they have heard from God however extraordinary it may seem.
- Always live in openness and reality with children. They can detect hypocrisy better than adults.

Chapter 13

Living in Two Worlds

I want to encourage you to walk in two worlds simultaneously with eyes and ears open to the Spirit of God and at the same time to the normal, ordinary, human world in which we live. It's practising the presence of God; it's becoming spiritually aware and sensitive at all times. Romans 8:14 says:

> *'Those who are led by the Spirit of God are the sons of God.'*

It's living in a faith dimension. Most people are blind and deaf to the supernatural world, but God is looking for a people, a prophetic people, who will walk as Jesus walked, and who will live in these two worlds concurrently.

Elisha, a man of two worlds

Elisha was familiar with two worlds, but he had a servant who was not! The king of Aram was at war with Israel, and Elisha was constantly warning the King of Israel of the next attack with such accuracy that the King of Aram thought there was a spy in the camp. In 2 Kings 6:8–17 we have the amazing story:

'Now the king of Aram was at war with Israel. After conferring with his officers, he said, "I will set my camp up in such and such a place."

The man of God sent word to the king of Israel: "Beware of passing that place, because the Arameans are going down there." So the king of Israel checked on the place indicated by the man of God. Time and again Elisha warned the king, so that he was on his guard in such places.

This enraged the king of Aram. He summoned his officers and demanded of them, "Will you not tell me which of us is on the side of the king of Israel?"

"None of us, my lord the king," said one of his officers, "but Elisha, the prophet who is in Israel, tells the king of Israel the very words you speak in your bedroom."

"Go, find out where he is," the king ordered, "so that I can send men and capture him." The report came back: "He is in Dothan." Then he sent horses and chariots and a strong force there. They went by night and surrounded the city.

When the servant of the man of God got up and went out early the next morning, an army with horses and chariots had surrounded the city. "Oh, my lord, what shall we do?" the servant asked.

"Don't be afraid," the prophet answered. "Those who are with us are more than those who are with them."

And Elisha prayed, "O LORD, open his eyes so he may see." Then the LORD opened the servant's eyes, and he looked and saw the hills full of horses and chariots of fire all around Elisha.'

Elisha's servant needed to have his eyes opened, and I believe it is the same for the Church of God today; we need to have our eyes opened. One of the reasons for writing this book is to encourage you to cry out to God for a sensitivity to the unseen realm of the Spirit.

Abraham was called *'God's friend'*, and in Genesis 18:17 it says:

> *'Then the LORD said, "Shall I hide from Abraham what I am about to do?"'*

God was about to destroy Sodom and Gomorrah. He told Abraham what He was going to do, and Abraham was able to intercede and plead with Him to change His mind. Eventually God agreed that if there were ten people in that city who were righteous He wouldn't destroy it. Unfortunately, there weren't ten people.

The NIV Study Bible note says:

> 'Because he was now God's covenant friend, God convened his heavenly counsel at Abraham's tent. There he announced his purpose for Abraham and for the wicked of the plain – redemption and judgement. He thus even gave Abraham opportunity to speak in his court and to intercede for the righteous in Sodom and Gomorrah.'

God spoke to Moses face to face as a man speaks to his friend. Enoch, another of the old patriarchs, walked with God and he didn't even die. He walked with God so much, it would appear that he eventually walked right into heaven!

These were ordinary, real men, but they had found a dimension in God which we need to find, of friendship, intimacy and accountability.

Hold on tight!

Some years ago I had what I consider to be a very important dream. I was standing on the edge of a forest and could see little pathways entering the forest. Running alongside the edge of the forest was a railway track symbolising a predetermined way of life. I could see it stretching into the distance, parallel lines with sleepers in between.

As a child I used to walk along the railway track to get to school and I remember what it was like to trudge along the sleepers stepping from one to the other. It was very predictable; it was hard to get a rhythm going. You had to watch your feet most of the time, or you were likely to trip.

In my dream, I saw a motorbike appear on the edge of the forest with a young man at the controls. He was extremely attractive. I didn't see his face, but was immediately aware of his vitality and his energy. He was wearing a denim shirt and he said to me, 'Come on, jump on the back.'

I had a choice, 'Did I want to stride this boring railway track or to jump on the back of this motorbike and explore the unknown narrow paths?'

I jumped on, and we set off into the woods. It was exciting, exhilarating, we were ducking under branches, laughing, I was holding on very tight – I had to. The driver knew where he was going and was enjoying giving me the thrill of my life.

In my dream, I was asked a question 'What would you prefer? To walk down the predictable railway track or to ride pillion on the back of my bike?'

At that moment I realised that Jesus, the driver of the bike, was giving me a clear choice.

Really, I had no option. I knew that the exhilarating ride, hanging on to Jesus, was the only way I wanted to go and so replied, 'Take me with You, teach me how to ride with You, teach me how to walk with You, teach me how to hang on to You, teach me how to trust You, teach me how to be Your friend.'

The Message, says:

> *'Walk with me and work with me – watch how I do it. Learn the unforced rhythms of grace. I won't lay anything heavy or*

> *ill-fitting on you. Keep company with me and you'll learn to live freely and lightly.'*

I know that I am talking about something unusual. Those whose eyes have yet to be opened may not understand it. Sometimes we, as believers, don't know how to communicate to others what is going on in the spiritual world and sometimes we are not very wise.

Did she fulfil her potential?

Some years ago our eldest son Craig was running a young people's group. There must have been 15 or 16 youngsters whom he taught to listen to God and who were highly prophetic young people. Some of them are now serving the Lord in far-flung places in the world.

I distinctly remember one girl, who naturally flowed into the way of life that I am talking about; she was so full of vitality and energy and spontaneously shared her faith with everyone. In her personality she was a very warm-hearted, friendly girl, but beyond that the dimension of the Spirit of God made her even more attractive.

I hadn't seen her for many years, and I had been told that she had ceased walking in the supernatural. Imagine my surprise and delight when I bumped into her in the centre of Wales, I knew this was a divine appointment, and she asked me to visit her, which later I did. She is now a woman in her early thirties, with a child and a business to run. I asked her if she was still walking with Jesus and she said she still loved Him, occasionally went to church, and acknowledged that the same anointing that she had was now on her young son. Sadly, she had gone through some difficult circumstances and was no longer walking in the prophetic dimension of those earlier years.

'What went wrong? How could we have helped you

more? Why did you lose it all?' I asked her, to which she replied,

'It made me different and I couldn't hack it.'

I found myself so incredibly sad when I heard that statement.

I thought, 'Yes, it does make us different.'

Yet Jesus was different, but totally magnetic to the people around Him; they loved Him, He was so much fun to be with, they invited Him to the wedding feast. He wasn't a dismal Jimmy who just put the mockers on everything. He was the man who brought life and vitality to every situation. He was accepted at the Pharisees' house, while at the same time the prostitutes felt at home with Him; they knew He didn't judge them, and that they were touching reality.

I've thought a lot about this young woman who had a similar charisma. I realised we failed to train her how to be wise. There is a time to speak and a time when not to speak; there is a time when we are casting pearls before swine if we talk about this spiritual world to people who have no understanding. There is a cost to carrying the anointing of God, and it requires allowing Him to change our character and build maturity into our lives; swimming against the tide and not being swept along by the crowd will inevitably make you different.

In the past I've been guilty of being unwise myself. After my mother died the opportunity arose for me to join my sister from Australia and for both of us to stay with our sister in South Africa. We three siblings had not been together in many years, so it was a unique occasion. My sister in Australia loves me. She thinks I'm a little out of the ordinary, but she knows where to come if she needs help. There were aspects to my way of life, which I had spoken too openly about, and certainly things that my children had communicated to her, which made her feel very uncomfortable. God's supernatural provision was one of them.

Her husband worked very hard; he spent long hours providing them with an income and maintaining their standard of living. We had been involved in full-time ministry for 25 years, and she felt that because we didn't have an employer, or a set salary, then perhaps we were skivers, and did not really work for our living. Quite the opposite was true, but she had not been able or willing to understand.

During our time in South Africa I overheard her in a conversation with my niece that was very critical of me. We often criticise things we don't understand. I was feeling very sad and alone that night. I prayed and asked the Lord to help me keep loving and giving, and not close myself off, because if people criticise you, there is the tendency to shut down and not communicate.

The next morning as I was getting up, I heard my two sisters laughing. They called me to join them, and my elder sister said, 'Listen to what happened to Audrey last night.'

She had a dream and in this dream she saw a man come into her bedroom and just as he was about to hit her on top of the head with a stick she shouted, 'Oh God, help me. I'm sorry I've been so horrible to Joyce.' Then she woke up and discovered that the bedside lamp had fallen over and hit her on the head! As they were laughing about this, I said, 'Yes, you were pretty horrible. It would be good to talk about it.'

Later that day we were able to go for a walk together. We cleared the air and she was able to tell me of the things in my lifestyle that she didn't understand. God gave me an opportunity to sort out our misunderstandings, but I do recognise that we have to be careful about what we say; we have to set a watch on our mouth and a guard on our tongue, lest we cause confusion or offence to those who don't see things as we do.

Perhaps there was once a time when you walked closely with the Spirit of God, but you've stopped listening, or you might have made a decision to block off this side of your life.

In Revelation 2:5 it says *'Do the things you did at first.'* If in earlier times you knew the reality of listening to the 'heavenly counsel', but now have stopped, then go back, get off the boring railway track and hop on to the pillion seat of Jesus' motorbike and you'll have so much more fun.

We can get so entangled with our sick and stupid culture. God knows that very often we don't listen, except in emergencies. He doesn't want the world around us to squeeze us into its mould; He wants us to live in touch with heaven.

There are times in all of our lives when we have to evaluate where we are. I had such a time recently when I was in Ghana. Whilst I was there God began to correct me and speak to me in depth about my listening skills. In fact He told me that it was time to write this book; it was time to challenge both myself and other people about the degree to which we listen to the Spirit of God.

I could have been in danger of jumping off the motorbike and going back onto the railway track because it is the easy option. But I repented and I have been doing the things I did at first.

Important points

- You are living in two worlds at the same time, listen both to the natural and the supernatural.
- As you look at the people and circumstances, look beyond the superficial and seek to see what God sees.
- Use what you see and hear wisely, to help you to pray and act with wisdom and faith. Don't be too quick to blurt it all out.
- Choose the motorbike ride, hanging on to Jesus as He leads you through the adventure of life.

Chapter 14

Listen and Live

Your ability to hear God could save your life. It is essential that you train yourself to listen to the Holy Spirit; you could find yourself in a situation where you are the only person who has the ability to hear God. He might use you to save the lives of others, who perhaps at that moment are not able to hear from heaven.

A miraculous escape

I heard this story first-hand from Andrew Thomas and his sister Beryl who are second-generation missionaries in Rome. The Apostolic Church in Wales sent out their father W.R. Thomas to Italy in the 1930s, where he and his wife pioneered in evangelism and church planting in central Italy.

Days before Italy entered the Second World War, an uneducated, but strongly prophetic church member received a clear warning from God for this family. With certain trepidation she came to W.R. Thomas and delivered the message, 'God has told me that you must leave Italy today and go back to your own country.' The Thomas family treated this warning seriously; they were experienced in listening to the voice of God. They immediately packed some belongings and left Rome that same day, heading north by train towards the French border. At the border their passports and papers were examined and their escape blocked. Italy had entered the war on the side of Germany, and as British citizens they were now enemies, and would shortly be due for internment. They were sent back to Milan.

The hot-line between earth and heaven was very active! God clearly spoke to W.R. Thomas and instructed him to return to the border on the next train. A different guard was about to repeat the previous scenario, but as he looked down at the children and thought of his own family, his heart softened and he allowed them to cross the frontier into France. God's schedule is always perfect. On this second train, they found themselves travelling with the son of the British Ambassador to France, and upon arrival in Paris they were immediately taken to the embassy. The next morning they were put on a train for the Channel, which was the last that left Paris before it fell. The only ferry available was going to the Channel Isles; they went aboard with relief and gratitude to God. It was again one of the last boats that got through. They had used all their money, and the hotel owner in Guernsey, a stranger, loaned them the cash for the final leg of the journey. It started with a word from God, it continued with the hand of God, and they arrived back in Wales only by the abundant grace of God. Their schedule had been timed to the second; delay would have meant imprisonment or death.

This same prophetic lady was again used to save the lives of a whole church congregation. Easter was approaching; everyone was looking forward to worshipping together on Easter Day. At the same time God was speaking to this lady, and she approached her Church leaders with a word from God. 'The Church is not to meet indoors this Easter Sunday, you must select a place in the countryside and worship there.' Again the word was received, was soon passed from mouth to mouth, and so that little congregation gathered in the woods. As they stood and praised God beneath the open sky, bombs were falling on the building where they normally worshipped. A word from God had rescued them from certain death.

An ocean rescue

The Apostle Paul was a prisoner travelling by ship from Crete to Italy. It was too late in the year to be sure of an uneventful journey. After the traditional time of fasting in late September, the early October weather was notoriously unpredictable. A text note in NIV Study Bible says, 'The Romans considered sailing after 15th September doubtful and after 11th November suicidal.'

Before the ship left port Paul warned of danger ahead, but the centurion and the pilot preferred risk to overwintering in an unsuitable harbour, and the voice of the majority decided to sail on. Consequently 276 men found themselves aboard a ship that for fourteen days was pounded relentlessly by gigantic waves, and blown like driftwood by hurricane force winds. The sky was dark by day and starless by night, navigation was impossible and 275 waited for certain death, while one waited for heaven to speak. What he heard saved their lives. An angel gave Paul clear instructions from his God, which he spoke out to the ship's company. He was given both practical instructions and promises of safety. Their obedience to these directives was vital. This time they listened and despite losing the ship, everyone on board was saved. The whole drama and loss could have been avoided had they listened and obeyed the first time. God had already told Paul he must face trial before Caesar and no natural disaster or hell-induced storm would stop that. You can read the full thrilling account in Acts 27.

Rescued from certain death

At the time when all of Eastern Europe was under communist

rule, many Christians experienced extreme persecution. There was a demonic hatred from many communist officials towards Christian pastors. It was a real clash, the kingdom of darkness versus the Kingdom of Light.

One night, in the former Republic of Yugoslavia, a pastor was travelling on a motorbike to a little gathering of believers out in one of the villages. As he journeyed he heard a voice inside say, 'Stop your motorbike' but he wasn't absolutely certain that it was God and kept on going. A very short time later the engine of the motorbike just cut out for no apparent reason. He tried repeatedly to get it going and as he pulled off to the side of the road, he thought, 'Well, I should have stopped. There may have been some reason.'

It was not a road that normally had much traffic, but as he waited on the side of the road he saw the lights of a lorry coming up behind him. As it came past the headlights of the lorry illuminated a thin strong wire stretched across the road between two trees at head height. It was hardly visible, but had he been riding his motorbike it would have caused certain death. The wire had been put there to decapitate him. The lorry not only illuminated the wire, but also cut through it.

This young pastor started to worship as he realised how God had preserved his life. As he recovered his composure, after his near death experience, he kicked the starter on his bike and it immediately sprang to life. He continued his journey thanking the God who speaks and acts on behalf of His servants.

The petrol bomb

During the time we worked with Colin Urquhart and were living at The Hyde in Sussex we had gathered for a Tuesday morning celebration to meet with God, to worship, to receive His word. The room where we were gathered was packed to capacity. My husband, Charles, had already begun the meeting, and some of the late arrivals were waiting outside. He was praying in a normal way when suddenly he began to pray loudly and take authority over every spirit of darkness and evil and began to quote a word from Isaiah, *'No weapon formed against you will prosper and you will refute every tongue that accuses you.'* He had become aware of a tremendous sense of evil. As I stood in the hall I thought, 'What on earth is going on? Why is he suddenly praying so strongly, so seriously?'

One of those waiting was a young woman who had been involved with a satanic cult, and was at that time living with us. She had been away for a few days and had now returned. She had, unknown to us, just visited her former cult friends, who sent her back to destroy The Hyde and the people who were trying to rescue her from their clutches. They had given her a petrol bomb, but as Charles began to pray, the bomb began to leak. It was hidden in her trousers and suddenly it began to drip liquid onto the floor. Someone spotted it and hastened her into the toilet, thinking she was having an accident. Once in the bathroom, the plot was revealed as the reek of petrol filled the room. The Spirit of God had, yet again, foiled the enemy's scheme.

Be very vigilant

On our return from Ghana, I felt impressed by the Spirit of God that we were to cover every single part of our journey. We were to pray about every minute detail. We prayed about the car and over all the mechanical components. (Not a bad idea in Africa!) I was impressed to ask God in detail what time we should leave and what time we should arrive. He also spoke to me about possible terrorist activity at Heathrow Airport. In fact, so urgent was the impression that I was getting from the Lord that I sent a text message to Charles saying, 'Be very vigilant.'

He likewise felt impressed that he must particularly guard his journey and had the sense that there could be danger at Heathrow. There were no incidents, the journey was successful and we returned safely, because we listened to the voice of the Spirit of God. I do believe we are entering increasingly dark days when we will need to be more vigilant in listening to the voice of the Spirit of God regarding our safety, and we will need to teach this to our children.

September the eleventh

There are many remarkable testimonies of those who escaped the tragedy of September 11th 2001 because of God's voice. Clear warnings came in dreams, there were alarm clocks that didn't ring, trains that were missed or delayed. Many had a strong sense that they should not go to work, and others through illness stayed at home. But at the same time hundreds who died were believers. Can every danger be averted? Have Christians who have died tragically simply failed to listen?

Only God knows the answer to those questions, but many people will testify to having received warnings they did not heed and wished they had. However, those who have walked the valley of the shadow of death need comfort and compassion not judgement. At present we see in part, we know in part, but one day we will understand fully. When Jesus was asked to comment on tragic accidents He focused on the eternal. In Luke 13:1–5:

> *'Now there were some present at that time who told Jesus about the Galileans whose blood Pilate had mixed with their sacrifices. Jesus answered, "Do you think that these Galileans were worse sinners than all the other Galileans because they suffered this way? I tell you, no! But unless you repent, you too will all perish. Or those eighteen who died when the tower in*

> *Siloam fell on them – do you think they were more guilty than all the others living in Jerusalem? I tell you, no! But unless you repent, you too will all perish.'*

Jesus reminded us that we all need to be ready to face our eternal destiny. Those who have experienced painful bereavements may have many unanswered questions, but take comfort that those who have a personal faith in Jesus are, *'Absent from the body, and present with the Lord.'* Jesus said to the repentant dying thief on the cross, *'Today you will be with me in paradise.'*

God's word to us from 1 Peter 5:8–9 is:

> *'Be self-controlled and alert. Your enemy the devil prowls around like a roaring lion looking for someone to devour. Resist him, standing firm in the faith.'*

But the Word of God also says that if we listen we will live. Proverbs 1:33 says:

> *'Whoever listens to me will live in safety*
> *and be at ease, without fear of harm.'*

But there is a condition, for in the previous verse it says,

> *'The waywardness of the simple will kill them,*
> *and the complacency of fools will destroy them.'*

Important points

- God is concerned for the safety of His children.
- Listen for God's warning as you travel and go about your daily life.

- Don't resist the delays and frustrations, they may be part of God's safety plan for you.
- We are living in days when we need to be alert and vigilant.

Chapter 15

Two Ladies with 'L' Plates

That is exactly what we were, two mature ladies, who had walked with Jesus for many years, now stepping into the unknown. We were in Ghana at the invitation of a young pastor from the north of the country. Pastor Alex was part of a church-planting organisation, and our mandate was to encourage new churches; to preach the gospel in three different centres; to heal the sick and set the captives free. It was my first time in Ghana and I was accompanying a long-standing friend, Angela Young, who was making her third visit. We didn't know any of the details of our schedule, but would find them out as each new day unfolded. God made it very clear that we were in Ghana at His command, He was going to talk to us in a new way and we were here wearing 'L' plates.

We were in rural Africa, in the most primitive situation that I personally have been in. Our guesthouse was, by European standards, very basic; but it was adequate, we had electricity (most of the time), a bed and running water. It would have been luxury for the local people. A cold tap, bucket and cup provided a blissful makeshift shower, when we were sticky, dusty and hot.

The practicalities of daily life were certainly an interesting challenge, but God had brought us here for a quite different adventure. This 'two-man' team had come to learn how to totally rely on 'heaven's voice'. We were on the front line, out of our comfort zone, facing situations like those described in the book of Acts. On the day we arrived in Ghana, God spoke to me from my daily devotional book, it quoted 1 Corinthians 6:17 from the Amplified Bible: *'But the person who is united to the Lord becomes one spirit with Him.'* It *went on to say, 'If you have united yourself to God by receiving Jesus as Lord, everywhere you go today . . . God goes too!'*

We were going into the unknown. I reassured myself by saying 'I am united to the Lord, I have become one Spirit with Him, everywhere I go today, God goes with me, God is in me, His power is in me, His wisdom is in me, the victory of God is mine.'

I have been travelling in ministry for many years, normally with my husband Charles, and in most situations we would be given conference themes, details of the programme and all that was needed to feel at peace, but here we were with no idea of what lay ahead of us. We had to hear our instructions from God; we had to learn to pray together in an entirely new way.

I have become used to hearing God on my own. I check out what I hear against the Scriptures, and it's a 'me and God' situation. Now Angela and I had to learn to trust God to speak to us together, and accept the specific things each was hearing from the Lord.

An audience with a king

On our first day Pastor Alex arrived shortly after breakfast with a surprise invitation. The king had asked to see these white ladies who had come into his province. We were somewhat overawed by the whole experience, extraordinary customs and strict protocol. He seemed both interested and puzzled by our presence, but as we talked he relaxed and said that we were welcome in his kingdom. As we left his palace he made a strange statement, 'I reluctantly give you the keys of my kingdom, you can go anywhere, do what you've been sent to do and you will be safe.'

After lunch and a short rest, we joined together to pray. Almost immediately Angela had a vision of an angel with keys in his hand. We understood from the angel that the keys were to lock and unlock different situations, and that these keys spoke of authority and purposeful action. Later we realised how flattered we had been by our visit to an earthly ruler; now the angel's appearance reminded us that we were being handed greater authority than anything found on earth. It shook us out of any complacency that we might have had, and made us realise that we needed to have our eyes and ears tuned into heaven. We needed to spend time everyday seeking God.

Why the 'L' plates?

We were learning to preach the gospel to people living in 2002, who had never heard about Jesus and knew nothing about God the maker of the universe, the Father of Jesus. Their gods were idols, ancestors and fetish stools. Witchcraft, curses and fetish rituals were a normal part of life. Fear ruled and was at times tangible. Disease, poverty and hunger were all around.

How was it possible to communicate the gospel to these people? God knew we needed to hear His specific instructions. He had promised before we left England that He would tell us what to say and how to say it.

So each afternoon we would get before God and ask him questions, 'What do you want to do tonight? What do you want us to speak and testify about? Are there any words of knowledge that we need to hear?' This was a new experience; we would worship, use the gifts of the Spirit, especially tongues and interpretation. We asked God questions, He asked us questions. When preaching we couldn't use notes or even read from our Bibles, because we never had sufficient light. It all had to come from our hearts. How well did we know the Scriptures? Had the Holy Spirit imparted enough to our hearts so that we could simply trust Him and let it pour out? We were utterly dependent on God. It was exhilarating, simple, satisfying and we saw God in action.

Each night we would leave our prayer closet and go out to the villages with a small and dedicated group of local believers – to be church. We would find a central place, string up some lights, and try to get the amplifier working! We then began to praise and worship, follow our instructions and see God act. The first night 25 people responded to the call for salvation and we saw amazing healings. We had received a word of knowledge that God was going to heal limbs and joints. The word was given; an older lady who couldn't bend her knee hobbled forward, we prayed and God healed her. She went wild with joy and excitement, she leaped, danced and praised God, and every subsequent night she walked over 2 kilometres to the meeting, testifying boldly and joyfully to what God had done.

One night God had told Angela to speak on forgiveness and broken relationships. Later we discovered that the place where we were preaching was notorious for family feuds. There were many people who were living close to their relatives but had not spoken to them for years. Eight men responded to the invitation and not only met with Jesus, but each wanted to confess their sins, receive forgiveness and the power to resolve these longstanding feuds. We had been unsure about this message and were questioning whether we had really heard God, but thrilled when we saw the response.

One day there was the funeral of a 32-year-old man. The whole town had turned out for the event and afterwards were drowning their sorrows, as the alcohol flowed freely. The sense of evil was tangible and pervaded the already heavy atmosphere. This was the town where we were due to preach for the next two nights. It was the only time during our visit that I had to battle with fear, and so we turned to prayer. God immediately reminded us of the time in the Bible when Samaria was under siege and the enemy camp was emptied because they heard the sound of a heavenly army. We took this as our direction and prayed that a heavenly army would go out and drive every demon out of town.

In the evening as we stood at our preaching spot in the centre of town, the fear and demonic oppression had gone and we knew our prayers had been answered as people were saved and healed.

We were learning the vital importance of being sensitive to God as He sharpened our listening skills day by day. However, as we prayed with the pastors we realised they had fallen into the habit of simply praying loudly in tongues, all together, for a long time; but we could not detect any real evidence that they were listening for God's directives. God showed us that we needed to teach them to listen while they prayed. So we began to mentor them and demonstrate the things that we had so recently learned, first with one pastor and his wife, then with others.

As we reflected on how we had learned to listen when faced with such difficult decisions and impossible situations, we understood how much in the past we had relied on experience and expertise in doing God's work. Did we preach a different gospel in Ghana? Are the people any different? Isn't there as much ignorance in Western Europe? Isn't there as much idol worship and darkness, as much poverty and disease? Our veneer of materialism covers so much – but underneath there are similar fears and feuds. We in the West need God's instruction just as much to enable us to know how to bring the gospel – in God's way. God will speak here too, as we wait before Him in prayer.

I returned to England changed and committed to listen to His voice as never before. Committed to pray with my husband, my friends, my church; determined never to lapse back into operating out of experience or rote.

Shortly after I had returned we had an appointment with a young couple who are leaders in our church and we just said to them, 'You know we could talk all morning, but let's not do that, let's just decide that we're going to hear from heaven.' What an exciting two hours we had.

I then went to lead our church prayer meeting. We would consider ourselves to be a people who move already with a prophetic anointing and that our aim is that our praying would be heaven down rather than earth up. But even there the Lord wanted to sharpen us up, because He was saying, 'Come near and listen.'

In Ecclesiastes chapter 5 it says,

> *'Guard your steps when you go to the house of God. Go near to listen rather than to offer the sacrifice of fools, who do not know when they do wrong.*
>
> *Do not be quick with your mouth,*
> *do not be hasty in your heart*
> *to utter anything before God.*
> *God is in heaven*
> *and you are on earth,*
> *so let your words be few.'* (Ecclesiastes 5:1–2)

> *'Therefore, stand in awe of God.'* (Ecclesiastes 5:7)

Important points

- It's fine to wear 'L' plates, there will always be much to learn.

- Even in familiar situations we need to listen to God's agenda.
- As we learn to listen, let's teach and encourage others to do the same at every opportunity.

Chapter 16

There Is Always More

You may be at the beginning of your walk with Jesus and have only just begun to listen to the voice of God. It is of the greatest importance that you realise that He wants to speak to **you**, find you listening and ready to obey.

Some of what I have shared may seem advanced or perhaps for you unobtainable. This is not the case; God will never ask the impossible, but wants us to seek Him with all our hearts and press on to greater things. As you progress in this life of listening, God will encourage you, but He will also stretch you. There is no limit to God, your adventures of faith are ahead of you, and you have a lifetime to reach out for more.

A famous mountaineer, who had scaled many of the world's highest mountains, but kept climbing, punishing himself, was once asked, 'Haven't you achieved enough?'

'While there are still mountains to climb,' he answered, 'I will keep on climbing.'

Can you identify with his motivation? Unclimbed mountains challenged and provoked him. There was an inner longing to face the challenge; he could never be satisfied with what he had achieved as long as there were unscaled summits.

So much more

Similarly, when seeking after God, there's always more. His ways are past finding out, and yet the search goes on. He challenges us to seek Him and when we think we have found Him, we discover there is more, and always will be. I do see, yet there is still more to see. I do hear, but there is yet more to hear. I do understand some of the ways of God, but there is more.

God is limitless, both knowable and unknowable at the same time. The Scriptures assure us of this, in Jeremiah 29:13:

> *'You will seek me and find me when you seek me with all your heart.'*

Song of Songs 3:3–4 expresses such longing:

> *'... "Have you seen the one my heart loves?"*
> *Scarcely had I passed them*
> *when I found the one my heart loves.*
> *I held him and would not let him go.'*

Romans 11:33 says:

> *'How unsearchable his judgements,*
> *and his paths beyond tracing out!'*

Those who do seek God still find Him

I personally am greatly challenged by people who have pressed into God and know Him more intimately than I do, people who have experienced more of His love and have seen more of His promises fulfilled. I know that God has no favourites and He will reveal Himself to all who will earnestly seek Him.

I am stirred by David Hogan, a missionary in Mexico, who seeks God with a prayer and fasting lifestyle. He has seen God raise more than 300 people from the dead, thousands of people saved and healed and many hundreds of churches established.

Jesus said in John chapter 14:12:

> *'I tell you the truth, anyone who has faith in me will do what I have been doing. He will do even greater things than these.'*

I desire to see greater things in my life. I reflect on detailed instructions God gave to Moses on Sinai, and the strategy given to Joshua to take the city of Jericho, and how Daniel solved the impossible situation of having to interpret a dream whose content was unknown, how he enlisted the help of his friends, and after personally seeking God he received understanding, both of the dream and the interpretation. He was then able to say to King Nebuchadnezzar with confidence:

> *'... but there is a God in heaven who reveals mysteries. He has shown King Nebuchadnezzar what will happen in days to come.'* (Daniel 2:28)

I am personally outraged when I hear reports of psychics helping the police to locate missing persons, by occult power. I long for the day when the 'seers', the prophets of God, will be called on to give heaven-sent revelation. This was Daniel's testimony in Daniel 2:22:

> *'He reveals deep and hidden things;*
> *he knows what lies in darkness,*
> *and light dwells with him.'*

God sees and knows everything, no bird falls to the ground without Him knowing. Certainly, when blood is split, it calls out. He knows, just as He did when Abel's blood cried out to Him. To whom can He reveal His knowledge? Who is listening?

There is a cost

Intimacy and commitment go hand in hand and those who desire this lifestyle will find it involves nothing less than total, uncompromising commitment to Jesus. Our personal comfort could be challenged in terms of misunderstanding and loneliness. People we thought were friends may reject us; we will be too radical for them. We will begin to understand what God feels about this world, and there will be a cost as we translate His pain into intercessory prayer. Once you have tasted of the new wine of the Spirit, the living water of revelation, there is no going back. At one time when many were abandoning Jesus because following Him was too challenging, He asked the twelve disciples, *'You do not want to leave too, do you?* They replied, *'Lord, to whom shall we go? You have the words of eternal life'* (John 6:67–68).

Daniel 11:32 says:

> *'... but the people who know their God shall be strong, and carry out great exploits.'* (NKJV)

I think of pioneers who saw Him who is invisible, and because of that did the impossible; they withstood opposition, mockery and other injustices. Whenever men and women receive a commission from God there will be mockers and scoffers; Noah experienced the mockery, but he survived the flood. Moses faced criticism from his own family, but he carried on with his commission from heaven, and saved a nation. Nehemiah faced opposition and ridicule, but still rebuilt the walls of Jerusalem.

Prayer with fasting

When there is urgency to seek God many will withdraw to *the desert, or the lonely places,* where fasting will be added to the season of prayer. Fasting sharpens your spiritual ears; it helps to set aside the bodily demands in order for the spirit to become stronger. In a large part of the Western church it appears radical; in the church of the Third World it is normal. Prayer and fasting become vital as the battle lines are more clearly drawn, the spirit world more easily recognised and the demonic realm more tangible.

Food is a necessity, but many in the West have made it a god. When you live on a diet of beans and rice on a daily basis, food doesn't have the same compelling attraction as it does in the West. Whenever you meet powerful men and women of God you will usually find they have a lifestyle of prayer and fasting, of being alone with God and with a greater 'given-ness' to the spiritual than the physical.

Pioneers

As soon as he was saved, the young pastor we were working with in Ghana was led into lonely places where he began to fast for periods of time as he sought God for his future. We regularly travel to Burundi where we are involved with African Revival Ministries, a nation-changing group born out of prayer and fasting, as was David Hogan's ministry mentioned earlier. Behind every revival there will be many seeking God with prayer and fasting.

Not under law

You need to get your directions from God as to when to fast, and when to feast. It can become an activity of the flesh, if we think we can bend God's arm by fasting. Those who have a prophetic anointing may well select certain times for prayer and fasting, as a means of sharpening the prophetic gift. There are many good books on the subject, suffice it to say there are different ways to fast; for some people it's a Daniel fast where you abstain from specific things at a particular time in order to seek God. For some people it's a day a week of prayer and fasting. For others it's simply missing a meal before an important event, and some will fast for as much as 40 days. You only need to do what God is saying, if God hasn't told you to do this, enjoy feasting!

Revolutionary revelation

A young pastor, Kong Hee, in Singapore, was directed by the Holy Spirit to purchase land near the Malaysian border on which to build a centre for his fast growing church. Many attempts had already been made to buy buildings and land, but without success. There was great excitement at the prospect of a new permanent building, so you can imagine the disappointment when after purchasing the land permission was refused to build beyond two stories. High-rise buildings are the norm in Singapore due to shortage of land. They needed a building with at least six floors to house their ever expanding work. Had they mistaken God's direction when purchasing this land? What could they do?

Time was set aside to fast and pray and hear God's instructions. As they listened, God gave creative ideas and they were granted permission to build below ground. The completed building has two stories visible and rest are below ground; much of the technology used was quite revolutionary, but Holy Spirit inspired. Architectural students from around the world are constantly visiting this exciting new centre.

The Holy Spirit also knew that land which appeared 'off the beaten track' when first purchased would be within the fastest growing suburb of Singapore and by the time the building was in operation, buses and trains would be serving this area.

God has no limits

Intercessors will tell of adventures in God where they went, by their spirits, to other parts of the world and saw in detail things He chose to reveal to them, so that God would have men and women interceding for situations that He wanted changed.

Norman Grubb's book *Rees Howells, Intercessor* recounts incidents that happened during the Second World War where the course of history was changed because people saw in the Spirit and prayed.

Others have had visions of heaven, similar to those described in Revelation, individuals walking with their God and doing exploits. God's great desire is to have a people who will know Him, who will listen to Him for themselves, their families and our nation, people who will understand that when two or three are gathered together as believers, Jesus is in the midst, He wants to be acknowledged, welcomed and listened to, just as we would if a close friend was in our home. We would not exclude them from our conversation, we would value their contribution and that is what Jesus wants when we gather together.

When we meet in our local church congregations God wants to speak. He wants to be given freedom to say and do what He wants. So often we squeeze Him out and no one asks, 'What does God feel about what we are doing today?'

We have so much to learn about heavenly protocol, and only as we recognise the awesome presence of God will we approach His throne with humility and boldness, to listen and to obey, to worship and to wonder at the privileged relationship we have been given.

A disturbing experience

I hope this book has disturbed you as well as encouraged you to keep pressing in to God, to keep listening, and experimenting. There is no 'one right way' to walk with God – your journey will be different from mine, the way you hear will be personal to you. Commit yourself today to obey the prompting of the Holy Spirit in the small seemingly insignificant things of life. When he says, 'Check this.' 'Do this now.' 'Phone this person.' – do it! As you obey the whispered promptings, you will grow in confidence, you will learn not to dismiss feelings, impressions and intuition, and will come to trust your teacher, God's Holy Spirit. He seldom tells us why we are to do something. We usually find out after we have been obedient. Having sensitised ourselves by obedience in the small things, we will not argue when we need to obey a word that may make the difference between life and death.

If we are really serious, Paul's words will resonate in our hearts when he said in Philippians 3:12–14:

> *'Not that I have already obtained all this, or have already been made perfect, but I press on to take hold of that for which Christ Jesus took hold of me. Brothers, I do not consider myself yet to have taken hold of it. But one thing I do: Forgetting what is behind and straining toward what is ahead, I press on towards the goal to win the prize for which God has called me heavenwards in Christ Jesus.'*

John the Baptist prepared the Jewish people for the first coming of Jesus. He was a prophet with an Elijah anointing, and he turned the hearts of the fathers to the children; he prepared the people to recognise Jesus. God is looking for that sort of prophetic people, not another John the Baptist, but His whole Church saturated in the Holy Spirit, a people with a prophetic anointing who will prepare the way for the second coming of Jesus.

We need to be those who will live with a radical lifestyle, a lifestyle of holiness, a lifestyle of obedience. A Korean pastor, David Yonggi Cho, who has the largest church in the world, was once asked the secret of his success to which he replied, 'I pray and I obey.'

We as the people of God

- Need to pray,
- Need to listen,
- Need to obey.

Books by Joyce and Charles Sibthorpe

Can You Hear God? by Joyce Sibthorpe
126pp. – £4.99 plus p. & p.

Help Yourself to Health by Charles Sibthorpe
96pp. – £3.99 plus p. & p.

Authority by Charles Sibthorpe
192pp. – £4.99 plus p. & p.

The Workman's One Year Bible Plan
£1 including p. & p.

The Workman's Two Year Bible Plan
£1 including p. & p.

Available from Living Waters Church

No. 24 Old Street,
Clevedon,
N. Somerset
BS21 6BY

Or purchase from our web site

www.living-waters.org.uk

Visit our web site for regular news, features and messages that will encourage faith.